ALSO BY ABIGAIL THOMAS

Getting Over Tom

An Actual Life

Herb's Pajamas

Safekeeping

A Three Dog Life

Thinking About Memoir

What Comes Next and How to Like It

A Memoir

❯❯❯❮❮❮

ABIGAIL THOMAS

SCRIBNER

New York London Toronto Sydney New Delhi

🔥

SCRIBNER
A Division of Simon & Schuster, Inc.
1230 Avenue of the Americas
New York, NY 10020

First Scribner hardcover edition March 2015

SCRIBNER and design are registered trademarks of The Gale Group, Inc.,
used under license by Simon & Schuster, Inc., the publisher of this work.

For information about special discounts for bulk purchases,
please contact Simon & Schuster Special Sales at 1-866-506-1949 or
business@simonandschuster.com.

The Simon & Schuster Speakers Bureau can bring authors to your
live event. For more information or to book an event, contact the
Simon & Schuster Speakers Bureau at 1-866-248-3049 or
visit our website at www.simonspeakers.com.

Manufactured in the United States of America

1   3   5   7   9   10   8   6   4   2

Library of Congress Cataloging-in-Publication Data is available.

ISBN 978-1-4767-8505-9
ISBN 978-1-4767-8507-3 (ebook)

The author is grateful to the editors of the following magazines for publishing,
usually in different form, pieces of this book: *O, The Oprah Magazine*;
Tin House; *Sonora Review*; *Open City*; *Drunken Boat*; and *The Ocean State Review*.

For Chuck Verrill

I

UNBREAKABLE
CONNECTIONS

Painting, Not Writing

I have time to kill while waiting for the sun to dry, and I'm mulling over the story I spent years writing and failed to turn into anything, trying not to be depressed. Nothing is wasted when you are a writer. The stuff that doesn't work has to be written to make way for the stuff that might; often you need to take the long way round. And if you're writing memoir you're bound to discover things about yourself you didn't realize before, may indeed prefer never to have known, but there you are: progress of some sort. Still, years. That's a long time to get nowhere. The story was about a thirty-year friendship that had a hole blown through it, but somehow survived.

So instead of not-writing, I am painting. I'm not a painter, but I make paintings anyway. I use glass and oil-based house paint, which is toxic, and which you can't buy just anywhere anymore. It's being phased out in favor of latex, which doesn't stick to glass, and acrylic, which I haven't tried. Stacked on my garage windowsill are seventeen quarts of the stuff in various primary colors, in case the whole world stops selling it.

I love the oiliness, I love how it spreads on the surface of the glass, how tipped at an angle it rolls and drips, and merges. I love how one color overtakes another on the downward slide. I use about a tablespoon of orange to make a sun, and I have four quarts of this color. I figure it will last me till I die. Anyway, I can't put the sky on until the sun sets, and this orange, this molten fire, takes forever.

Write a Book

This is some years ago. "What can I do for you?" I asked Chuck. He was depressed. So was I. He had hepatitis C. He had been diagnosed with stage four cirrhosis. It was not a rosy picture.

"What can I do for you?" I asked again. I figured if it was good for him, it would be good for us both.

"Write another book," he said.

"What kind of book?" I asked.

"Make it fiction," he told me. "You'll have to lie sooner or later. Might as well start off on the wrong foot."

"I don't know where to begin," I said, wondering if we were talking about the same thing.

"Start in the middle," he said.

"I always do," I answered. "What book am I writing?" I asked, to be sure.

"The one about me," he said.

"The one about the three of us?"

"Yes. That one."

"I don't know," I said carefully. "I don't know anyone's story except my own and I don't even know that."

"It has to end when one of us dies," he said, "and that should be me."

"I don't know," I said again. I didn't say, *You're not going to die, don't be silly.*

"Make it up," he told me.

Yes I Was

You were never depressed," Chuck tells me now. "*I was depressed.* You were always trying to talk me out of it."

"I was too," I say. "I was *totally* depressed." We are standing on the curb at Forty-First and Broadway. It's quarter to seven at night, March 2010. We have known each other for thirty-one years. He is a literary agent now, I am a writer.

"You're the least depressed person I know," Chuck says, as the light changes.

"How can you even say that?" I ask, but stop there. This is a ridiculous argument. Getting me into a ridiculous argument is a specialty of Chuck's. Like one of those Chinese puzzles where the harder you pull the tighter your fingers are stuck in that straw tube, only Chuck does it with words.

So I give up. He smiles.

"How's your hip?" he asks, offering me assistance as we start across the street. I have arthritis.

"Oh shut up, it's *fine*," I say, taking his arm.

When It Started

We met in 1979. I was thirty-seven; he was twenty-seven. I had been twice divorced and had four children, Chuck was happily married and had none. I was working at a publishing company as the slush reader, which meant I handled everything that came without an agent. He took over my job because I had been promoted to editorial assistant. Slush was the only position lowlier than editorial assistant, but instead of a cubicle, it came with its own small office. It had a door that closed and a window that opened. The walls were lined with bookcases, the bookcases filled with manuscripts, some read, some waiting to be read. I would read and return, read and return, putting aside for further consideration the few too interesting to reject out of hand. The trouble was that after a week I regarded those partially read manuscripts with the same lack of enthusiasm one might feel for somebody else's half-eaten sandwich, which made me so guilty I began to resent them, so I'd box them up and send them back without reading another word.

The big gray desk took up most of the space.

It was my job to train him, but all I wanted to do was make him laugh. He was good-looking and nervous, an interesting combination. "Open everything that comes without an agent," I told him. "Open everything addressed to the president of the company, or the editor in chief. And then make it go away. If anything is good, you can show it to a real editor. And you know what you never want? You never want to encourage somebody who tells you she has been writing since she was five years old."

I may have been a little intense, because I remember his face twitched, out of anxiety maybe, or the pressure of having to pay close attention in such a small space. We were both smoking our heads off, the window wide open, the door shut.

We took out a manuscript dedicated "To my wife and children whom I love very much, and to the memory of all those who have died by choking." I'm certain we took a look at the book (who could resist?), but all that remains is the dedication.

When I had nothing pressing to do, I helped Chuck with the stuff that piled up on his desk. "Listen to this," we'd say, in the weeks that followed, waving a manuscript around. And there would be something hilarious, or terrible, or sad. We particularly loved the letter from a man who had managed the produce section in a big supermarket on Long Island. He wanted to write a novel about his experiences in the retail grocery business—he had seen so much—but didn't know how to begin. He was so earnest. He thought we really *were* the editors in chief. "Just tell me what to do," he wrote at the end. "I'll do anything you say." We laughed. We weren't laughing out of meanness. We weren't unkind. We laughed because it was all so hopeless.

"It's not about making the cosmic joke," Chuck said the other day. "It's about getting it."

The First Night

I remember the first night Chuck came to my apartment, but not why. We never saw each other outside of work. He was married, I had kids and boyfriends. When I ask him now, he thinks maybe he had lost his keys. "Those were desperate times," he says, laughing. "Desperate times call for desperate measures."

I don't remember any desperate times. I remember maybe rain. I was roasting a chicken. My youngest daughter, Catherine, sat next to him on the sofa. She had a new Donkey Kong game and they played it while I peeled potatoes. Now and then I looked at them, thinking, *How nice.* Their heads touching. I was forty. He was thirty. My daughter was nine. Her hair was always tangled in the back. Did he let her win? I doubt it.

Earlier, before Chuck showed up, she had ushered me into the kitchen, telling me she had a present. *What could it be?* I wondered. It was a bowl of sliced peaches and cream, she had prepared it carefully all by herself, and she stood next to my chair and watched as I ate every bite. "Do you want some more sugar?" she may have asked, and "No, this is perfect," I may have answered.

"When I grow up, I want to be just like you," she said, and my heart filled with gratitude. I was flattered when she grew up and people said we looked exactly alike.

Five Years

Five years Chuck and I worked together, and then came the day I was promoted, this time to a position of semiresponsibility. No longer could I say what I loved and what I didn't. No longer could I work on something handed to me, or the occasional thing they let me buy. From now on I'd have to back up my taste with sales figures—I'd have to go to meetings and sales conferences. I'd have to admit that publishing was a business, not just a lot of laughter and excitement and fun. I would have to be cautious, and caution was never my strong suit. There I was, clinging for dear life to the bottom rung of the ladder and they were prying my fingers loose.

I found myself in a reflective mood. Goodness, I hadn't read a book for pleasure in years. I missed it! How I missed it! The very act of reading had become not unlike the experience of having somebody's brights in your rearview mirror all the time. I decided maybe I'd like to go to school and become a social worker, or a nurse, or a teacher, or a massage therapist, or . . . it was vague, but the upshot was I was going to beat it.

"How can you leave me here?" Chuck asked, but he was fine. He already knew everything I would never learn about the business end of things. I didn't think of it as leaving him. We were best friends.

But we weren't in each other's pockets anymore. What had been effortless now took some doing. I was one hundred blocks uptown. We had seldom gotten together outside of work. I realized friendship required attention, like a houseplant. We talked on the telephone. We kept it going. And after weeks went by, when we returned to each other, the friendship was always there.

I spent the next six months working for a college counselor in a school for rich people's children. I found myself asking them, all these young men and women who wanted to be lawyers and plastic surgeons, if any of them didn't want to drop out of school and join a rock 'n' roll band. Maybe start a little family? Their faces were blank.

Then an agent called Chuck for a recommendation. She was looking for someone to help with the reading, and he suggested me. The agent was someone I knew and liked and respected. I leapt at her offer. Yes, I said, yes, yes, yes.

A few years later I convinced Chuck that he should be an agent too. He came, after some discussion, and we were together again.

When the real agent went away for the summer, Chuck and I were left in charge of the office. We noticed after a day or two that the phone had stopped ringing. In fact the phone never rang from one day to the next unless it was our boss, checking in.

"Maybe this is what's called 'going out of business,'" Chuck said, and we laughed heartily.

We sat around inventing things. We invented desk ornaments like the little trolls some people had, only ours would be action figures incapable of action. "Inaction figures!" There would be Torpor and Languor and our favorite, Stupor. Our fortunes would be made! We even had one in honor of Stephen King called Bangor. It was a brilliant idea. But how to put them into production? Here we were stumped.

Then the real agent came back and the phone picked up again.

Reproducing

Chuck's first son, Sam, was born December 18, 1983. I gave him my signed copy of *The Winding Stair*. My first grandson, Joe, was born to my eldest daughter, Sarah, on December 18, 1984. He was tiny, no bigger than a fryer in the chicken department. Sarah's second child, my grandson Sam, was born in 1986. Chuck's twins, Hannah and Joseph, were born a year later.

Hannah as a little girl fell in love with the color pink. She told her father, "I want a new *pink* daddy."

Are You Two Together?

We went reluctantly to publishing parties. We either arrived together or met there, one of us waiting outside smoking until the other showed up before venturing in to where the people I thought of as grown-ups were talking knowledgeably about I knew not what. Once inside, we stuck close. One night we were introduced to a large woman sitting in a comfortable chair holding court, like an amiable spider.

"Are you two together?" she asked. I shook my head.

"No, but we gave it some thought, didn't we?" said Chuck, which surprised me.

"I'm his mother," I said.

The Mess Is All

I can never make the same painting twice, not that I want to, I guess. Still, it would be nice to make a better version of something, or try it in different colors, but I never remember how I did it, or when I fiddled with it, or what went down first. A lot depends on how long you let the paint set before interfering. I drip and fling and pour color onto the glass. Then I push the paint around. You have to have some faith. If it looks like nothing, if you think you've destroyed what might have been a good painting, keep at it. If you've scraped all but a few streaks away, chances are those streaks will suggest something else. Don't give up. Don't be afraid of the mess.

The process is a lot like writing. You start with a wisp of memory, or some detail that won't let you be. You write, you cross out. You write again, revise, feel like giving up. What pulls you through? Curiosity.

Married Again

When Chuck and I first met, I was in love with a poet. "I'm in it for the pleasure," I told my poet once, in a moment of bravado. The poet grinned at me. "I'm in it for the pain," he said. It ended sadly. The kind of ending where you wait together, holding hands and weeping, while off in another room, love slowly dies.

Another poet, good-looking and very intense, once asked me over lunch, "Abby. What do men want?" I was unable to answer. I said he probably knew the answer better than I did. "I want to be *scorched*," he said.

After several more tries, each affair ending badly, I decided maybe I was better off alone. *Well,* I thought, *I'll try this one more time, and if nothing comes of it, I'll be fine.* I put an ad in the respectable *New York Review of Books,* and waited. Among the letters sent to me was one in particular I liked, and there was something appealing about the handwriting. I can't explain it.

We met at the Moon Palace, a restaurant that used to be on Broadway and 112th Street. It was raining when I got there, and a man standing outside had a large umbrella. I remember thinking it was big enough for two. It was Rich. He turned to greet me. A handsome man.

Rich was nice. I don't remember what we talked about, except we talked about everything, but I do remember thinking when I got home, *My god, I've found the honeypot.* Thirteen days later Rich asked me to marry him, and I said yes. It was sudden, as love always is, and Rich suggested that my kids might want to meet him, to make sure their mother had not gone crazy. Sarah, Jennifer, Ralph, and Catherine approved. Catherine was the only one still living with me. Just as I was telling her what Rich and I were planning, the phone rang for her. "Can I call you back in ten minutes?" she said. "My mother's getting married."

At our wedding, Sarah said, "You look like a prince and princess from a very small and not-that-rich country."

It was a perfect description.

On our honeymoon, we ate grits and eggs and bacon and biscuits every morning, and I began to worry that pretty soon even my stockings wouldn't fit. I felt like a small soft avalanche lying on top of Rich. I mentioned it to him at breakfast. "I'm afraid you can't breathe," I said, mouth full of grits with cheese. "If I can't breathe," he said with a smile, "I'll just shift my position a little."

Oblivious

Rich moved into my apartment. In the first flush of love, I had not considered this would be hard for Catherine. She was sixteen. She was used to quiet evenings reading, and suppers of strawberry shortcake, our own ways. Catherine liked Rich, but she was not used to sharing her mother, or her bathroom, or the living room where suddenly a couple sat, not just her and her mother. This hadn't been her decision, nor had she been consulted, and really, what could she have said? No? Don't change my life? She was nicer than that, she wished me to be happy.

It was months later, when we were shopping for clothes, that I noticed how much weight she'd lost.

"Look at this interesting bone," said Catherine, pointing to a knob visible on her shoulder where no knob should be. I panicked, but Catherine wouldn't discuss it. I poured heavy cream into her tea. I added sugar to everything. Rich bought pork fried rice at the Cuban Chinese restaurant on Broadway, and left it on the counter for her every night. She would get up when we were asleep and eat it. Weeks later, I took her to Marvin's, she ordered eggs Benedict, and I watched her eat every bite.

Stories

I had written poems in the seventies, but the poetry dried up. When I tried to write words that went all the way across the page I got discouraged; "Who do you think you are?" I'd mutter, balling up the paper and tossing it into the wastebasket. "You're not a writer. Writers are unusual people."

Then one day somebody told me a story that stuck in my head. I wanted so badly to tell it. I was obsessed. For the first time, the story was more important than my ego, and after failing, I tried again, and then again. It was a mother-daughter story, and once I quit trying to write it in the voice of the woman whose story it was, and imagined me the mother, and the daughter one of my own daughters, it worked. The story got published in a literary magazine. I wrote another, it got published too. Now every time a good manuscript came my way at work it made me want to go home and write. Every time a bad manuscript came my way, it made me want to go home and write. Rich said, "Why don't you stay home and do your own work? I'll take care of us both." That's the kind of generous man he was. It was 1990.

I can't remember which story I showed Chuck first, but thank god, he liked it. When my whole book was done I gave it to him. "Would you be my agent?" I asked. He told me later he had read it on his back steps, and his wife heard him laughing and came outside.

"I thought you were working," she said.

Copping to It

What do we use? That's easy. We use everything. We have our eyes and ears open to snag the lovely and the harsh and the hilarious. There is ruthlessness to all writers. That first story up and grabbed me by the throat, and I was oblivious to the fact that I was stealing.

I had no idea I had done anything wrong until I ran into the woman whose story it was. She said she had seen it in a magazine. She congratulated me. I looked at her face, which was expressionless, and understood for the first time what I'd done. I was ashamed of myself. I still am, but that story turned me into a writer.

Workshop

But I wasn't writing all the time. Days, sometimes weeks would go by without my doing anything at all. I began to feel like something left too long in the vegetable drawer. Then I had the bright idea of starting a weekly writing workshop. There would be a point to me! I sent out a typed announcement to friends and people I'd worked with as an agent. Soon there were a dozen people wanting to join. Eleven women and one man. When the man found out he was the only one, he decided not to come. That was the start of the Tuesday Night Babes, a group whose core continues to this day, twenty-some years later.

I was terrified that first night. I vacuumed and dusted. I baked something. Then I sat around waiting for six-thirty wringing my hands. What would I talk about? How would it go? Who *was* I? At twenty past six Rich retired to the bedroom, giving me a reassuring kiss. "You'll be fine," he probably said. But how would I fill the time?

Everyone arrived. I told them a man had chickened out and we all had a good laugh. Think what he might have learned, we said. I gave everyone a piece of whatever it was I'd baked, and we were off and running. I have no idea what else I talked about, but I laid out the rules. Every week two people would have their work discussed in depth. Pieces would be handed out a week ahead, so we all had a chance to go over the work carefully.

I said I would give assignments, just for fun, and at the end of class whoever had done an assignment could read it aloud.

Several books came out of those assignments, including a wonderful book by Elizabeth Ehrlich, called *Miriam's Kitchen*. I
think the assignment had been to write two pages that included
an iron, a kitchen counter, and an egg-salad sandwich. Elizabeth
wrote two pages she called "How to Keep a Kosher Kitchen."
Her mother-in-law made egg salad the way her mother and her
mother's mother had always made it. She had been a refugee
from the Nazis, and she cooked everything according to tradi-
tion to honor the dead, to keep faith. I remember, I think, that
to make the counter kosher, she ironed it.

Catherine's Job

After college, Catherine was tossing around for a job in publishing when, lo and behold, she was hired by the same literary agency where Chuck and I had worked, where Chuck still worked, only now he was a partner. For Catherine this was like coming home. She had known everyone there for years, the office was small and friendly, the writers they represented were wonderful and varied. This was the perfect job for her. And what's more, it had a future! It was lovely for me that she was there. It was a little like being back myself. I imagined Catherine and Chuck laughing over the same kinds of things he and I had laughed at, getting excited about the same kinds of books he and I had loved. She worked there for five years. Sometimes I would take the subway down and have lunch with the two of them.

"Don't you just love her?" I would say to Chuck, and "Isn't he great?" I'd say to her.

Then, out of the blue, she quit. She loved her job! I could not believe it, let alone understand. She told me nothing of why, and it made no sense to me. But her father had recently died. All her young life she had been afraid because he was so much older than other fathers. Then he got sick and died.

She wouldn't answer my calls; every room I was in was a room she wanted to get out of. I thought I was failing her in her grief. One evening I persuaded her to meet me for dinner at an Italian restaurant we both liked. *My god, you are beautiful,* I thought, as she sat down. "I just want to know if you're all right," I said. For a moment it looked as if she might answer. "Mom," she began, but then she pushed her chair back and stood up. "I'm sorry," she said, putting her coat on, "but I just can't do this," and she fled.

It was Chuck I called for reassurance. After all, he had known her since she was nine years old. "I'm doing something terribly wrong," I said to Chuck, "and I don't know what it is."

"This has nothing to do with you," he said over and over. "You're a good mother. She loves you." He told me this as many times as I needed to hear it. Then one day he invited me to lunch.

It was 2000. The restaurant had cloth napkins and ice water and stiff menus. It felt like a date. He had something to tell me. He had had an affair, and he had separated from his wife. I wondered how I hadn't known something so important. He was serious, he spoke carefully, respectful of everyone concerned. I could tell it was important to him that I understand.

I didn't ask who the woman was. He'd tell me if he wanted to. "She didn't mean for my family to break up," he said. "She never meant for any of this to happen."

I talked about what happened to my children when I got divorced, and I got upset, remembering how they had suffered. I told him how my gentle son, Ralph, then no older than twelve, had comforted his younger sister when her father and I fought and divorced. I told Chuck what Ralph had said to her: "Don't worry. I went through this when I was your age too." Catherine was five years old.

Then I burst into tears.

It was an emotional meal. "Take care of your kids," I said. "Do a better job than I did." Chuck said he was doing his best.

The bill came, and he paid, and I thanked him. I was standing up ready to go, but he was still sitting down, his wallet lying on the table. He didn't move.

"What?" I asked. "What's the matter?" I sat down and reached across the table to touch his hand. He looked upset, more upset than I'd ever seen him. "What is it?" I asked. He shook his head. There was something he wanted to say and he couldn't leave without saying it, but he could hardly speak. "Abigail," he said, then stopped.

It took me a minute.

"Oh my god," I said. "Oh my god."

"It couldn't have been anybody else's daughter," he said.

The Sky

The sky doesn't come in this color. I had it mixed. It appears through thick plate glass as a wonderful lavender-gray. When the edges of the sun are firm, I can begin. I like a cloud or two, just wisps of things, and this is the only time I actually paint, plan, using my fingers to make a drop of white a see-through smear. The tangerine ball of a sun just blows my mind set in this color.

My First Reaction

Catherine and I were not estranged! The only part of this that had anything to do with me was that Chuck was my best friend and Catherine was my daughter. What a relief!

That Lunch

D o you remember that lunch?" I ask Chuck now. He is usually adamant about not being able to remember things.

"Of course I do," he says.

He tries to recall the name of the restaurant, but I don't care about its name.

"I remember you sat facing the window," he says.

"Was it hard for you to tell me?" I ask. I want to hear him say it.

"I remember you took my hand, and I was grateful," he answers.

Calling Catherine

I wanted to tell you myself," she said. "I wanted to tell you for such a long time. I didn't know what to do. I couldn't tell you and I couldn't not tell you."

The affair was over, so much of this was history now. I found it hard to catch up. This should have been none of my business. Love is love, after all, and I'm all for it. But because we were tangled up together, it became something done behind my back. What made me angriest was that my daughter was fired. She had broken up with Chuck, but his wife found out, and to try to keep his family together, Catherine had to leave. She never complained about this, never thought of herself as a victim, she had done what she had done. "It was all inevitable," she said. Chuck and his partner helped her find another job and he looked after her as best he could, still loving her, but the fact remained: he let her go.

And this had all happened a year ago. I was angry with Chuck, I didn't want to speak to him, but the anger made it possible to skip over the part where my best friend had slept with my daughter, and my daughter had slept with my best friend.

So I admit it came in handy.

Why It Took So Long to Tell Me

Catherine was afraid I would be angry with Chuck. Chuck was afraid I'd be angry with Catherine. This says something about all three of us, but I don't know what it is.

Forgiveness

Time has passed. I have metabolized this stuff, I think, but every once in a while it returns in its original form and towers over everything. Like grief.

I love my daughter, and I love my friend. Two people I love loved each other and still share great affection. They both love me. Forgiveness was never an issue. What is forgiveness anyway? It seems to me the only person you can forgive is yourself.

"Why does forgiveness irritate me so much?" I ask Chuck.

"Because it's the ultimate act of passive aggression," he says.

"Because it keeps sin alive," says my sister.

Forests

I love my forests, some more successful than others, my favorite being one I did on a big storm window. It took me a couple of weeks. I had it laid across two sawhorses, I kept scraping and dripping and flinging, turning it over to see what was happening. When I was finally done, and don't ask how I knew it was done, I didn't know whether I liked it or not for another week. I do like it. I love it. My son, Ralph, made a shelf for it on my living room wall. It's too heavy to hang.

Here's what I love about painting. It's not about words or voice or tone or point of view or narrative arc (perish the thought); it's about the way certain branches stick straight out from the trunks of certain trees; it's about the clouds that you can barely see as well as the ones that pile on top of each other; it's about the swoop of telephone wires and the shapes and colors of shadows.

A real painter recently told me that all artists want to draw telephone wires.

Complaints

People complained that, when Chuck and I were together, there might as well have been nobody else in the room. We were a pair, not a couple, but we laughed all the time. When I got married again, even Rich, who came upon Chuck and me as we were deep in conversation at Live Bait, felt uneasy, backing away. Later I asked him what had happened, why had he left?

"I felt like an intruder," my husband said.

"You're my *darling*," I said, but I knew what he meant.

"So what was it," I ask Chuck now, "that made us such good friends so fast?" I expect him to say that we laughed at the same things, or disliked the same people, or loved the same two lines out of a three-hundred-page manuscript.

"Neither of us had any ambition," he answers.

I open my beat-up *American Heritage Dictionary*. "'Ambition' comes from the Latin, meaning 'seeking votes,'" I tell him.

"So it has always been political," he says.

"Oh my god," I say, "exactly! That explains everything!"

Another Explanation

Maybe there are clusters of souls born again and again into the same repertory company, and with each new birth they play different parts in a different play. Or maybe it's the same play. This would account for those moments of *Oh! there you are!* After all, there are those people we like and dislike, there are those people we love, and then there are those we recognize. These are the unbreakable connections.

Telling My Husband

It was a month before I told my husband. Rich was the most moral man I knew, and I decided I couldn't afford his righteous anger piled on my own confusion. When I finally did tell him, he surprised me. "Poor Chuck," he said, "poor Catherine." Nothing more. No judgment, no righteous indignation.

I began to understand that it was not his anger I feared, but my own.

And then a week later, Rich went out to walk our dog and was hit by a car. He suffered traumatic brain injuries. He was never to be himself again. He was never to live at home again. This catastrophe drove everything else from my mind. Nothing else mattered.

I didn't miss Chuck. I didn't want to see him. Here's what I remember. I remember hospitals. I remember my husband's anguish and my own. I remember my children helping, and my friends helping, and my sisters helping. I remember my husband's daughter at my side. I remember one night coming home after weeks of long sad days with Rich and finding Chuck standing outside my building. "I'm taking you out to dinner," he said, "you need to eat."

I remember the shock of relief and gratitude when I saw him there.

Maybe it was too much to lose my husband and this friend.

A Close Call

Chuck took me to a house in the country for a respite. Rich was getting no better. This was all so long ago now, back when I had only one dog, Harry. Harry, who didn't come when called, didn't sit, stay, roll over, beg, nothing. I had tried to teach him "sit" once, pushing his rump down, but it offended him, and he walked away. Harry was an old dog, and I was a relatively new dog owner. I warned Chuck not to let him out. "He's a city dog," I said, "he will get lost and I'll never get him back." I sat on the lawn. Chuck brought me bacon and eggs and toast with lots of butter. He went back to the house for the coffee.

Halfway through my bacon, Harry came trotting jauntily past, tail held high, and disappeared immediately into the woods. Chuck had let him out. He was so sure it would be all right. But Harry was *my* dog. I jumped up to follow him, clambering over fallen trees and muddying my feet in swampy land, wailing. Harry came back on his own. If he hadn't, I'd've lost a dog, and I never could have looked at Chuck again.

Failure

I am trying to convince myself that failure is interesting. I look the word up in the *American Heritage Dictionary* to find its earliest incarnation, but it has always been just "failure." There's no Indo-European root meaning originally "to dare" or "mercy" or "hummingbird" to make of the whole mess a mysterious poem. I can find no other fossilized remains in the word. Humility comes along on its own dime.

"I don't know how to do this," I told Chuck, meaning the book I was trying to write.

"Turn it into a novel," he said.

"I can't write a novel," I said.

"You do it by evading the truth," he told me, and he wasn't laughing.

"I don't know what you're talking about," I said.

"It seems to me," he emailed me later, "that you start out with what you know or what you think you know and you work within those 'truthful' boundaries until you reach some sort of wilderness of not knowing, and then you find a way through until you see an end, or you find a way through until you find the end that you've already seen. It can work either way: running away from the truth, or running out of it."

I try to imagine the terrain. Where are the boundaries? I look around carefully.

They have all been crossed.

In a weak moment, Chuck offered to write his side of the

story. He planned to use my assignment of three-word sentences to describe any ten years of your life. I give it to all my incoming students. "Take any ten years of your life, reduce them to two pages, and every sentence has to be three words long." It's a good assignment. You can't hide behind a sapling. There are two examples that I've never forgotten. "Slept with Israelis. Needn't have bothered." And, "He was cute. I was clueless. It seemed right."

Chuck started with 1979, the year we met. He came up with two sentences: "She was funny. So was I."

That was it.

Not much help.

Making a Moon

When I make a moon, I don't attempt the craters and shadows. All I want is a big round moon because it's the best I can do, and because it does not involve knowing how to paint, only how to hold a stick still while the paint drips off, and because I love the way it looks. Sometimes I put a cloud down first, and the moon goes behind it.

"How do you get them so round?" Chuck asks.

"I drip it off a toothbrush," I tell him.

New Year's Eve

Chuck and I were going to have supper and go to the movies. We both hated New Year's Eve, but needed the company. Rich was in a rehab facility, Chuck was getting divorced. When he came by the apartment Catherine was there, getting ready to go out with her friends. She was working at a farm upstate called Green Chimneys. There were five young women tottering around on high heels. They were putting on makeup in front of the bathroom mirror, fixing each other's hair. There were shrieks and giggles. There were strapless dresses and one wig. Catherine was lovely, silly, distracted, young. In my company, like it or not, Chuck became a reluctant grown-up.

We all left together, Chuck and I and the gaggle of girls, and we walked up 112th Street to Broadway. The girls hailed a cab and climbed in, shouting good-bye. I noticed Chuck's face fall. Catherine hadn't asked him to join them.

Half an hour later my friend had disappeared, and in his place, sitting across the table from me, was a stranger. We were at Ollie's, bowls full of wet noodles in front of us. This stranger had nothing to say; he might as well have been sitting alone at this table. So might I.

Let's parse this: my friend is my daughter's former lover, and my daughter is the woman rejecting the man sitting across the table from me. What makes this intolerable is that I seem to have misplaced a friend and a daughter, or they have misplaced themselves, and now I'm angry with them both. We finished our dinner in silence. Chuck told me he'd changed his mind about the movie. He was tired. He disappeared into the subway at quarter to twelve.

A day or two later he called to tell me what I already knew— that seeing Catherine had upset him, that he hadn't wanted to inflict that misery on me, and so he'd bailed.

Maybe if the woman he loved had been someone else I wouldn't have been as angry. Maybe we would have talked about it, although he was never one to kiss and tell. But that night I was shut out of his world and, worse, shut out of my own, a world I'd put together, a world that contained my friend and my daughter.

Hadn't he seen the same girl I had seen? Laughing with friends? Tottering around in high heels? "She is too young for you," I snapped. It was unpredictable, this moment, but it was always on its way. "Grow up," I shouted.

After that, conversation was joyless. We no longer trusted each other. Chuck had been hurt by the scorn in my voice. I was alternately furious and numb. We were going to take a break from each other. Our friendship had become too complicated.

"Do you remember when we stopped talking to each other?" I ask. Chuck looks blank. "After that New Year's Eve?" He shakes his head. We are sitting in my living room with the woodstove cranked. It's winter again. I try to tell him what I remember. It's painful. The more I talk, the more depressed we both get. I wonder if he regrets having started this ball rolling.

"Remind me why you want me to do this." He doesn't say anything. I ask again. You have to be ruthless to get anything done in this racket. Finally he says he knows there will be things in it that will make him uncomfortable, but that it's necessary, it's part of the story. That's all I can get out of him.

But I can use it.

Wanting to Tell Chuck

The other day I came across something in an old diary. My badly injured husband must have thought he'd seen something over by the window, the kind of thing you see out the corner of your eye. He was in a hospital on Long Island, lying on his narrow bed.

"What is it?" I asked, seeing him distracted.

"I thought a bird had come detached from its shadow," he said.

It would have been Chuck I wanted to call. It's Chuck I call now.

I Can't Lose You

After months of silence, one of us wrote the other. "I can't lose you like this," the note said. We met for lunch. Our conversation was as careful as if we were ironing a shirt. It was not a success, but there was a reason we had been friends for so long, maybe it would unearth itself if we met again. It was hard work, like chopping wood, but we kept at it. Finally it was as if we climbed into two monster trucks and plowed over the rubble and crashed through the wall and came out the other side.

What I mean is we had the will.

Painting

With painting there's no doubt when it doesn't work. You don't hold it this way and that, hoping it will get better. Luckily, when you paint on glass, you can razor it off. Halfway through scraping off a bunch of apple trees, I turned it over, and there was the painting—a ghostly stand of birch. All I had to do was to enhance the accident. I love this painting now, with two red apples still glowing in the lower right-hand corner.

Just Name It

I made a forest of blue trees. Then I made another, smaller one. Then another, thinking myself on a roll, only this time I got the woodsy equivalent of a Sears family portrait. It was okay, you could see clouds and blue sky behind trees, but it was uninteresting. I should have known while I was making it—nothing surprised me except that when it was done it was dull.

I scraped it off, and since the paint had dried at different speeds, the razor skipped on its way up the glass, and made jagged branch-like things. Interesting, so that was my starting place for a new painting. Unfortunately, when it was done, I found I had reinvented plaid. Then Ralph came down for a visit, and he held it at a different angle, pointing out the tiny houses and the railroad tracks and high-tension wires and the orange lights in the factory windows. "Call it the Industrial Revolution," he said.

"Oh my god," I said. "You're right!"

That was the day he told me that washing my hands with turpentine was a bad idea. "That's *poison*, Mom," he said. We went to Houst and bought a big container of something orange that smells like PEZ. It works fine.

The Platonic Ideal

S o here I am banging away wondering what this connection to Chuck is all about, and all of a sudden I get it. At least I think I get it. The connection with him is a connection with part of myself, and it has to do with a kind of insatiable curiosity. I mean the part of me that gets connected to the rest of me when I'm connecting to him. The insatiably curious part. Only connect! Only connect! That's as far as I've gotten. It's a little indistinct, but I am excited.

Foolishly I tell him.

Here is part of his response:

"Sounds like the platonic ideal," he says. "Meantime," he says, and then puts Catherine's name in a Randy Newman lyric that has nothing to do with the platonic ideal. It is in very bad taste. *What's* wrong *with you?* I wonder, annoyed. Later I ask for a definition of "meantime." I already know the song. "I meant in the past imperfect tense sense," he writes. "I would say past perfect except it wasn't. I mean, it was past. But it wasn't perfect. And it was tense." Now I must look for my ancient copy of Plato's *Symposium*. I only read it once, sitting in the backseat of a Morris Minor while my parents drove around England. I was sixteen and didn't understand a single word.

The next time he calls I don't pick up the phone.

It occurs to me that there are two of him now—the walking-around dude with his own life, and the one I am talking to when I'm by myself. Sometimes the Chuck who calls me up isn't in the same mood as the other one. When the one in my mind seems realer than the one who's breathing and coughing, I begin to wonder if I'm making one of them up. Fortunately I couldn't make up one without having made up the other. I'm good, but I'm not that good.

Afraid

I have always been half in love with Chuck, but it's the top half. I love how his mind works. I love how he can take my fumbling for words for some idea and turn it into a coherent thought. I love how he makes me laugh.

Every now and again I'm afraid Chuck will fall in love with somebody and I will lose him. This comes from the worst part of me, the possessive part. I used to get upset if somebody I didn't like loved a book I loved. *That's* my *book*, I'd think. It's not that I don't want Chuck to be happy. I do. I just want him happy the way he is, but in a house closer to mine. He lives in Massachusetts. Sometimes I look through the *Woodstock Times* and send him real estate listings. He pretends to take them seriously.

The Possessive Part

Chuck's wife never liked me. We met at a ball game, when friends of Cork Smith, my old boss, had rented Shea Stadium for an afternoon. I am certain I was pushy about our friendship in front of her, and had I been in her shoes, I'd've hated me too.

I ask Chuck about that day. "I dropped a fly, hit a triple, and bunted in the winning run" is what he remembers, not that it was the day I met his wife.

Nothing More Than This

Chuck drives to Woodstock and leaves his dog with me for a day while he goes to a doctor's appointment. This is the redbone coonhound I got for him because he was lonely. Pojd (which is Czech for "come") is payment for all the good things and all the bad things Chuck has done.

After the appointment Chuck comes back and spends the night. I make that chicken thigh dish we both like (although it means fending off four determined dogs), and we stay up very late. The next day he hangs around until the afternoon; we are having a particularly nice time. Ten minutes after he leaves he's back, having forgotten something—the tickets to a game. Then he's off again. Twenty minutes later his car is pulling into my driveway again. *What is it this time?* I wonder, and decide to open the door saying "What, you came back to ask me to marry you?" which I think is a good joke, but before I can say a word, he flings his arms open and says, "Marry me!"

"Okay," I say, and I tell him what I had planned to say and we laugh, a little stunned at the coincidence. After he finds his cell phone (between couch cushions) and gets back in his car, he rolls down the window to say, "That was funny, the whole marry me thing, wasn't it?" and I say, "Yes, yes it was." We are both, I think, actually happy at this moment. It is nothing more than what it is, two friends who think of the same joke at the same time, but it's comforting to know that this is what we've always done, and all we have to do.

Scraping

The first time I scraped off most of a painting I turned it over and saw streaky white trees and a lot of Spanish moss. That wasn't what I'd planned, it was better than what I'd planned. The next thing I did was next to nothing, and when I was finished I had a swampy ghostly forest. It was my first favorite painting. It occurs to me that what I'm doing is reinventing pentimento.

Sex Again

I don't think of Chuck in a sexual way, except he is a man and I am a woman, and sometimes there is something in the air that adds spice to conversation. Sex isn't what I wanted from him, nor is it what he wanted from me, but it is something I'm aware of. Attraction isn't restricted to sex. One thing doesn't always lead to another. But it makes a nice hum in the background.

This morning I looked at an old photograph. It hangs on my wall, and it's part of the woodwork, but today I took it down to examine. It's a photo my daughter Jennifer took of our company softball team. There is Cork, a legend in publishing, and one day to be Catherine's father-in-law; there is an old boyfriend of Jennifer's, others I remember well. And Chuck.

Chuck can't have been much more than thirty years old in this picture, if that. My god, he was good-looking. These are the words that pop into my head, I can't help it: *you're like a great big candy bar.* Did I know that then? I must have. But I never broke him down into components: I never thought, *My god, look at that ass,* or *those shoulders,* or *that you-name-it,* the way I did the ones I wanted to sleep with. When I looked at him I saw *friend.* I'm standing to his left, a mess of blond hair and a smile. Maybe we'd won the game. He has a Brooklyn T-shirt on, I am wearing my denim skirt. I always wore skirts.

Chuck was captain because he could do everything. Since I could neither throw, catch, hit, nor run, he made me the pitcher, betting that sooner or later the opposing team would be impatient enough to take a wild swing. One afternoon we used a couple of ringers, one of them an old friend of his. He wore a bright orange T-shirt, his hair was black, and he had dark eyes and a beautiful mouth. He came to my house at midnight a few nights later carrying a Sara Lee cheesecake. "I couldn't think of anything else to bring," he said.

"I fell in love after ten minutes," I wailed. "What's wrong with me?"

Chuck was most helpful.

"You don't *slide* into love, Abigail, you fall," he said.

Chuck says we made out once. He remembers it was after a Twelfth Night party and I don't; I remember making out at a publishing party, he doesn't.

We had gone together, as we always did, only this time he went off in pursuit of a pretty woman, and by that time he was my best friend, so although I didn't want him to pursue me, I didn't want him to pursue anyone else when I was in the vicinity. I don't know how he knew I was upset, but he came looking for me, and what he said made everything all right for the next thirty years. Today I ask Chuck if he remembers that night, and he does, in great detail, minus that moment. He remembers me dancing with two men whose very existence I had forgotten. In the course of recounting the evening, he begins to wonder why he remembers it so well, since he hasn't thought of it since.

"Do you remember talking to me," I ask, "when I got upset?"

He doesn't.

"Wow. That's so interesting," I say, but I don't care. Once upon a time, when I was young, his forgetting might have rendered my memory meaningless. I no longer require so much from life.

"Maybe the thing I forgot is what makes me remember," Chuck says, which is why I love him. An entire novel could be written around that one remark.

Here's what I remember.

I remember a wide empty wall behind me. I remember lots of people dancing ten feet away. If I said I remember colored lights I would be making it up, but they were certainly there. And the music.

I think I remember seeing him walk toward me, but maybe not. I do remember him standing in front of me without saying anything, then shrugging his shoulders. I remember what he said. He said, "I love you. That's all." I definitely remember that, because of the "that's all." That was the part I loved. We kissed. Then he said, "But it's better this way, isn't it? This way we get to keep it." And so we have.

Triangles

Chuck and I were driving around in the dark. We were lost in the country somewhere in Massachusetts. It was pitch black and there was nothing but woods and winding roads and no streetlights. Not much moon either. We'd been trying to find our way for an hour. "We keep driving around in triangles," he said, and I had to tell him why I laughed.

Bad Memory

I have a bad memory. I have been trying to remember being young, which is hard because I don't feel old until I try to get up from my chair. Or when I look at the photograph Jennifer took of me sitting on a stool next to her twins, and really, from the back, it looks as if I have an open umbrella concealed under my skirt. *How did that happen?* I think, but, oh well, I was young once and slender and pretty and I made the most of it. It's somebody else's turn now.

I am remembering walking along Fifty-Ninth Street after work when I saw a tall elderly gentleman in a long black coat, a cape, maybe, leaning on a cane. I stared. There was something about him, as if he had just stepped out of a Charles Dickens novel and was looking around for an orphan to save. As my grandmother might have said, he cut quite a figure. Unfortunately, being a good New Yorker, I couldn't break stride and so sailed past, but every time I looked over my shoulder at him, he was looking at me. Then he was gone, vanished, I figured, into one of the buses that went wheezing past. I wondered who he might have been. I wondered what his story might be. I was still wondering when I came to the second red light and there he was.

"It's you," I said.

"What took you so long?" he asked, as if he had been waiting all his life.

I put my arm through his. He rented a horse-drawn carriage that meandered through Central Park while in the back, under a lap rug, we kissed. I can't remember what we talked about, or what his life had been, only the kissing, and thinking *Oh my god, don't die*, because he was in his late seventies, an age I no longer consider quite so old, coming up on seventy myself. I must have given him my number because we met once or twice more, and then as life would have it, he called too many times and I stopped answering. It was a sad trailing off, and I regretted it. I told my boss.

"You shouldn't have seen him again," Cork said. "It was a good story until then." He had the reputation of being a brilliant editor.

But I have never learned to edit my life while in the process of living it. For me, Cork's comment is as much a part of the story as the story itself.

But I can't remember the old man's name. What was his name?

I call Chuck. "Remember that old guy I went out with for a minute a thousand years ago?" I ask.

"Syl!" he says immediately. "Good old Syl!"

He remembers what I forget and I remember what he forgets. It's too late for either of us to make another old friend.

II

I DON'T GET TO LIVE
FOREVER

Sleeping with Dogs

I used to feel about king-size beds the way I do about Hummers and private jets and granite countertops, but over the past several years I gained three dogs and thirty pounds, and my old bed, a humble queen, just didn't cut it anymore. It was either lose the weight, lose the dogs, or buy something bigger.

I fell in love with this particular bed because it was handmade. It was designed originally as a rope bed, and Ralph spent a day outfitting it with wooden slats because I had researched rope beds and didn't want to sleep on anything I needed to tighten regularly with a special tool. The mattress I picked out is as high as a wedding cake. When I'm up there I am thirty-eight inches off the floor. I feel like the ruler of a small, rumpled country.

It is an exaggeration to say my nose grazes the ceiling.

Two of my dogs, Rosie and Carolina, jump up with ease, but my old beagle, Harry, can't make it. He was able to manage the other bed, but he had to back up to the wall to get a running start. Now there is no space left for a running start. This bed takes up the whole room, so I heave him up every night. I hope never to need a heave up myself. So far I am troubled only by arthritis, and if it gets worse, I can always ask my son to make me some stairs. I imagine covering them with red velvet.

My whole perspective has changed. When I lie in bed I am at eye level with the top of my bureau. I can see the photograph of a horse chestnut tree and a white chair beneath it, almost hidden by leaves, where my father liked to sit. I can see, I think, the charger for my cell phone, lost these many months. I am closer to the ceiling fan, which came with the house, and resembles something trying to resemble something out of an old saloon. It doesn't move the air around much, but makes a pleasant sound.

I love it up here.

The four of us sleep in a huddle. Harry dives under the covers toward my feet on the left, Rosie on the right, and Carolina on my (our) pillow. During the night, Harry gets out from under and arranges himself on top of the blanket; Rosie inches up to lay her head on my shoulder; and Carolina, who tends to start compact and neat, softens and unwinds, extended by morning to her full length. When I open my eyes, there is Rosie, her eyes already open, watching my face.

Sometimes I wonder if I might be missing something with only dogs for companionship, but then I think about mornings. First there would be the discovery that there is no milk for someone who takes it in his coffee. Then the likelihood of conversation. I want to listen to the mourning doves. I like to sit on the sofa with the dogs, stroking Carolina's silky chest, and Rosie's satin flank. Harry sits on my feet, standing guard. Suppose another person were here? What if he had opinions? What if he used the word "deconstruction" with a straight face? I remember asking Chuck to explain deconstruction to me again because I couldn't keep it in my head. We were walking past Hunter High School on Madison, and he began to talk about all those French people and then he gave up.

"It's just something to do," he said.

What if some man wanted to tell me how many feet from a dwelling a cesspool needed to be? What if he wanted to talk about the pros and cons of raising the mortgage rate? What if he wanted to talk about his *childhood*? Or worse, *mine*! I can put up with Carolina's barking because she'll stop for a treat (and because I love her so much), but people are different. You can't shut them up with the offer of a dog biscuit or a little piece of broccoli.

Lots of people in my somewhat leaky boat are on the lookout for a human companion. Not me. I have learned to love the inside of my own head. There isn't much I'd rather say than think. Of course for more than thirty years I've had Chuck. We've known each other so long that we don't have to talk, and when we do we don't have to say anything. When he asks me if I'd like to take a trip around the world I can say yes knowing I'll never have to go.

The Boy

The telephone rings. The last time I saw this person was 1955, when he was twelve and I was thirteen. He has called out of the blue, having just finished reading a book I wrote. He loves my writing and he has a nice voice. He reminds me that he had been so smitten and so shy back in seventh grade that all he could do to show his affection was ride past on his bicycle and throw candy bars at me. He is calling from his sister's house, and when we hang up, his sister says, "Next time, let *her* talk." And he calls me back to tell me that.

A week later he sends some old photographs: our combined seventh and eighth grades, our junior choir, his birthday party—a table full of kids whose names I've mostly forgotten. I am sitting to his left. "I was a boy and you were a woman," he writes on a sticky note attached to the photo. We played spin the bottle at that party, and when we were supposed to kiss, I refused. "I don't have to kiss you, I'm not going to marry you," is what he remembers my saying, and he was crushed, having secretly hoped we would get married. I don't remember any of this; it's like being a character in someone else's story. I stare at my thirteen-year-old face, but nothing is revealed. I am a stranger. I remember mostly anxiety, punctuated by bouts of self-righteousness. I decide not to tell him that in those days I was afraid I would murder my parents in their sleep with the barbecue fork. None of this seems important now. After spin the bottle we had a fight, and a day later he called to apologize. "I meant to say it was all my fault," he tells me, "but what came out was 'it was all my fart.' I didn't know what to do so I hung up."

I call Chuck. He laughs. Then he changes the subject.

"You only experience puppy love once," the boy (I can only think of him as a boy) tells me, trying to describe the sensation. "It's like being tickled," he decides. Do I remember Miss Lee's dancing class? Vaguely. He does. He remembers I was a foot and a half taller than he was. He remembers looking up at me wanting to say, "You are beautiful," but all that came out of his mouth was "You're tall." I look at his picture again. He is darling, he is innocent, but he is twelve and I am sixty-seven.

And then he sends me a mix tape, all rock 'n' roll, and I play it in my car on the way to the city. With the volume as high as it goes, I am listening to the Chambers Brothers singing "In the Midnight Hour"; I have one arm out the window, banging the beat on the side of my car. "I'm gonna take you, girl, and hold you/and do all the things I told you" could be coming from the mouth of a twelve-year-old boy who has no idea what he's talking about, but I do, and I'm doing eighty on the Palisades Parkway. I imagine myself in a ditch, car overturned, wheels spinning, and when the cops find me the only sign of life is coming from my CD player, "In the Midnight Hour," still cranked. *What was she thinking?* I imagine them scratching their young heads, wondering.

I call Chuck. "I've heard quite enough about this," he says, which surprises me, but I like that he sounds tired of it all, and not because it's boring.

The boy wants to come for a visit. Is there a hotel nearby? I tell him I have two extra bedrooms, if he doesn't mind the company of ill-behaved dogs. We make a plan. I call Chuck. I'm nervous. "He's in love with a thirteen-year-old girl," I wail, "and I'm sixty-seven. How can I lose fifty pounds in two weeks?"

"He's going to fall in love with you," Chuck says.

"Not a chance," I say.

But what if after all these years since 1955 it turns out we have been making ourselves into two people made for each other? I'm a writer, I'm curious: I want to know how the story turns out, but without living through it. I don't want to fall in love, but I want to see what happens if I do. I want the possibility of change, not change itself. I don't want to be filled with love, or longing, or desire, those emotional states I once pursued, but now think of as distractions from life rather than as life itself. I hate this feeling, I love this feeling, and that's why I'm painting.

These days I am painting apple trees, one after another—red apples, yellow apples, blue apples, silver. I have four paintings going at once, waiting for leaves and fruit to dry, and I am covered in paint up to my elbows. To see what progress I am making, I have to turn the painting over. This is tricky, especially if I am impatient and flip it while the paint is still wet enough to slide around, but it's also how I have the lucky accidents, how I discover that merging colors makes something better than what I'd had in mind. I can only do this kind of work by myself. I need to work myself into, then out of a mess. I need paint dripping and papers drifting and sliding; I need to make notes, lose things, I need to stay up late and go to bed early. I need to run out of milk, coffee, cigarettes. I need to burn with my nice hard gem-like flame, the one that gives off no warmth. Just as I'm on the verge of calling the boy from 1955 to tell him not to come, he calls to cancel. He has a complicated life. We discuss a rain check, but I am crushed. I am crushed and relieved in equal measure. I call Chuck. "What's that poem about the painted thing being better than the real?" I ask. I need backup for my new thesis that art beats life. Chuck refers me to Keats's "Ode on a Grecian Urn."

In the way back of my backyard are three real apple trees. Two of them are upright; one, after a long period of rain followed by a windstorm, has fallen on its side, but the branches still make leaves and blossoms and apples, which the deer eat right away. The biggest tree is back in the wild grass. High in its upper branches are scores of red apples, fat and glossy. I stand near where the tall grasses are often flattened by what I assume to be a family of sleeping deer, and this morning, for a moment, I wish I had the nerve to wade through, climb the tree, pick the fruit, but the moment passes.

Twins

Within six months of each other, my daughters Catherine and Jennifer had twins. Jen is single. We charged the sperm for Jen on my Visa. "All sperm is donor sperm," I told her. Instead of looking at IQs and College Board scores, Jen picked a nice-sounding man who loved dogs. It has worked out very well. Violet and Ralphie were born in August 2005.

Catherine is married to her childhood sweetheart, Tim Smith, Cork's youngest son. In 2006, when her twins were born, Chuck drove us to Philadelphia, and we visited them in the NICU. Augustus and Frederick. "We're raising dictators," said Tim. They looked like tiny sea turtles.

What with Ralph and his three daughters, Sarah with four sons and a daughter, two sets of twins bumped me up from eight grandchildren to twelve. I tend to think of this as my own accomplishment.

Abby's Book

On my computer is a file, "Abby's Book." I opened it the other day and read the first sentence: "I sit in a chair, one of those uncomfortable hospital chairs, the ones that have a sort of cushioned seat, and a back that stands straight up. I watch my mom in the hospital bed, scared that if I turn away from her, she will disappear."

For a moment I wonder when I wrote this. What a great opening sentence. Then I read further and realize this is my granddaughter Abby's writing. She was fourteen, I think, at the time. I am impressed.

The Realization

I
t is the end of a summer, the loveliest time of year. Years have passed since Catherine and Chuck's affair. Catherine is visiting from Philadelphia with her family. They are going to stay for two weeks. But she leaves the milk out and the lights on. She doesn't make her bed. She doesn't wipe the counters clean enough. I am irritable. The second night, her little kids are up until eleven, and I go upstairs without saying good night, closing my bedroom door.

The next morning I start to say, as evenly as I can, that eleven is too late for the kids to be up in the living room. We are outside on the deck, she is picking up a few toys. "Couldn't you take them upstairs a little earlier?" I suggest.

"Well, Mom," she says quietly, "I think we're going to go home." I look at my daughter. She holds a truck in one hand, a bunny in the other. Her face is sad and angry. The kids are running around, laughing their heads off. I love them so much.

"But why?" I ask. My heart is breaking. What is happening? They have been here only two days.

"I don't feel welcome here," says my daughter. "I haven't felt welcome for a long time."

And suddenly I realize how upset I am, and that I have probably been angry for years. How could she have done this thing with Chuck? is a question I have never asked myself, or her. We need to talk, it is desperately important that we talk, but a friend is on her way to see me, and she has driven almost a hundred miles. I have to meet her, and I have to leave now.

"Promise me you won't go until I come back," I say, but one look and I know I'm not reaching her. "Promise me you'll wait," I say, "we need to talk," and the whole time I am gone I am afraid I will come home to an empty house.

But three hours later we are in my car, sitting in the parking lot behind the hardware store. I don't know how to begin, I don't want to say this badly. I choose my words carefully. I don't want this to be about blame.

I tell her that writing this thing, this whatever it is, is affecting me. I've realized I never let myself be angry with her, but that what happened had hurt me. I tell her it was like losing my daughter and my best friend. I tell her how hard it was, stuck in a mess I didn't make and couldn't fix. My voice shakes. She listens quietly, intently.

Even before she speaks I see how upset she is. She makes no excuses. Her regret is fresh, her remorse real. She tells me how sorry she is and I know it's true. She says this is the first time she's realized how hard this was for me too. Ten minutes later I don't care if she leaves lights blazing all day and all night. I don't care if she leaves the milk out, or even if she drinks out of the bottle itself. She is my daughter again, and I am her mother. We are balloons floating in the blue sky.

Yard Sale

Fall, and all my kids were visiting. A guy down the block was selling his dead mother's stuff and I asked my kids to see if he had any old picture frames with glass, or windows, but they came back shaking their heads. Evidently it was sad over there. All morning people got out of their cars, looked around swiftly, and drove away.

I tried not to think of the detritus of a mother's life laid out on card tables for sale, and no takers. I wondered what my kids would do with my collections of anything and everything. I hope they don't feel guilty if nobody wants my barrel staves or my pieces of iron or the run-over windshield wiper, but there's nothing I can do about it.

I think about death because death is inevitable, but what else is coming? My mind draws a blank. The words "plan for the future" actually make me laugh out loud. The future is a moving target, completely unpredictable. Like the past.

I didn't know I never thought about it until I had coffee in the city with a woman who thought about it all the time. She worried that her future had shrunk. She worried about her health, although she looked fine to me. She lay awake at night with these worries.

"Don't you?" she asked. I was staring at her beautiful shoes.

"No," I answered, wondering if this was a failing. "I never think about the future at all."

"I worry about what would happen if John got sick or I got sick, I worry how we would manage."

I don't worry about my husband, the worst that could happen to him already happened. He was hit by a car in April of 2000, and sustained permanent brain damage. Seven years later, January 1, 2007, he died. Grief is different from worry. I don't want to remember what it was like before, eating muffins and reading the paper together on the porch. I don't want to remember him planting the wild grasses that he loved, or the way he smiled at me, or his generous heart. I don't want to remember walking down Broadway holding hands. I am still shocked by what happened. I am used to never getting used to it. But grief overtakes me in the coffee aisle, or sweeping the porch, or smiling at the dogs, catching me unaware. Grief is not a pleasure, but it makes me remember, and I am grateful.

The worried woman was only a few years older than I am. Maybe seventy-five brings with it the gravitas I lack. When we parted, I allowed myself to feel sorry for her, a woman wasting a perfectly good afternoon worrying about something that might never happen. *Well, the death part will happen*, I reminded myself, but before this line of thought could go any further I was distracted by a figure clad entirely in gold walking toward me on Fifty-Ninth Street. I took it all in, the gold hat with a golden feather, gold jacket and pants, gold boots, golden gloves, a gold lorgnette, and a golden mask that covered his or her entire face. *Oh, New York*, was all I was thinking, *I love you so much*.

Junkies

Ralph and his girls—Quinn, Justine, and Renny—went to another yard sale and brought me back a painting. The background is a bunch of blue buildings, the foreground is a man (or possibly a woman) screaming. "Nana will love this," Justine had said, excited. I love that she knows me so well.

We are all junkies. We stop when there is what we like to call "good garbage" by the side of the road, or sticking out of Dumpsters. Ralph used to come back with more taken from the dump than he had deposited. I pick up bits of iron that look interesting, Catherine stops for run-over reptiles and adds the bones to her collection, Jennifer drags furniture into her car, and Sarah does a lot of eBay. Well, we have all done a lot of eBay.

Somehow it is more interesting to find something beat-up and handled than to get it new. My bureau drawers are stuffed with god knows what, and my daughters always go through them when they are here. It is a compulsion. My theory is that they are looking for the secret, the answer, the explanation for everything.

The Children's Zoo

Chuck and I ate lunch together almost every day. This was probably twenty-five years ago, but I remember it clearly. Something about the city skyline made me melancholy. Central Park South always depressed me—too many awnings, all those fancy doormen, all those tourists. Chuck ate barbecue potato chips and drank Coke; I ate a cheese sandwich. There were bald spots in the grass. A pretty young woman nearby was reading a big book, we wanted to know what it was. "*Principles of Accounting*," Chuck said, after a good squint. Hmm. Not what we'd thought.

The smell of horse manure wafted over on a breeze from the hansom cabs parked on Fifty-Ninth Street, and sometimes we could hear the clopping hooves. I asked Chuck if he was filled with longing the way I was. A chronic longing I didn't understand.

He nodded.

"What is it," I asked, "what are we longing for?"

"There is only the longing," he answered.

One lunch hour we were too depressed to sit down. We wandered over to the Tisch Children's Zoo, where we came upon three little pigs eating shit. We patted them, smelled our hands afterward, and moved on to goats. Chuck noted that goats were particularly dumb, but delicious roasted. I told the goat never mind and it started eating my skirt through the fence. It was a pretty day.

On the way back to work I bought a paper snake on a stick for a dollar and Chuck grabbed it away, and practiced the wrist action, getting the snake to strike in the air all the way back to work, cheering us up.

Jennifer's Blog

Jen started a blog a few years ago. It's called *Cautionary Trails*. Sometimes I'm in the blog, and every once in a while I say, "Oh, can't you put in the part where I made a cake?" and she answers, "Mom, you write your *own* blog." Ugh. Another writer in the family. She writes about the difficulties of being the single parent of twins, of feeling off to the side, of being disorganized. She writes about what she feeds her kids (elaborate delicious dishes hiding all kinds of healthy things like carrots and kale in biscuits and pancakes), and occasionally she writes about men. Here's one of my favorites:

the man in the store

We are visiting my mother. It's where my kids are happiest. It rains and then it's sunny and then it rains again. This after-noon when they were drawing Ralphie called out, "Mommy, how do you spell 'boring'?" I thought he was writing in his diary but he was making a joke poster about Violet. They're having a good time.

I drove to the place with the handsome man for a sandwich. I do not have a crush on him but damn he's good-looking. He asked me if I was related to Abby and I answered yes, I'm her daughter. As I spoke a chip fell out of my mouth. He kept talking and things kept falling. A pepperoncini from my sandwich, a potato chip onto my lap, something onto the floor, and so on. I held my stomach in and hoped my arms weren't looking too chubby.

Even when there's no interest on either side one's coordination completely disappears in the presence of beauty.

Jen always calls when she's finished another piece and reads it to me. I never pretend to love something I don't. She trusts me. I think she is a marvelous writer. Sometimes she says, "Mom, why is it that only you and I laugh at this?" I am proud of her.

Time

I think about time differently since I got to be this old. I think of each moment as a big La-Z-Boy, or perhaps a hammock, and the only direction is a little back and forth, or side to side. For this I need peace and quiet, and I eschew all outside stimulation. Perhaps this is why the future escapes me.

I love my twelve grandchildren, but they function (as do their parents) on linear time. When they visit, I mobilize. I bake my cookies; I bake ginger snaps and chocolate chips and cornmeal sugar cookies and shortbread. I bake big chewy chocolate cookies. I give everyone two at a time. Why not? You only live once. I notice that with small children everything is a beeline to the next thing. No time for lolling about, which is what I do best. I call myself a writer, but I am stone lazy.

I appreciate that the advantage of getting old is you don't want to mess around anymore. In order not to want what I don't really want, I am careful about the movies I watch and I play music only in the car. When I watch a movie I don't want to cry or be moved or enlightened and I don't want to be turned on. There are movies I cannot watch, or watch more than once. I saw the one about Woodstock, and it took me almost two years to get over Viggo Mortensen. I bought the DVD because I loved it so much, but I never opened it. It has sat on the shelf for four years. I like movies with good guys and bad guys and a lot of big guns. I do not want anything stirred up that I can't handle by myself.

When the twins came over Christmas I baked cookies and roasted sweet potatoes and chickens and simmered my stews. I loved it when the babies climbed into my lap. After a week of two sets of two-year-old twins having a really good time, I decided it was time to leave the house. "Time to flee" were my exact words to myself. I realized that my gynecologist had died fifteen years ago and thought it prudent to find a new one right now this minute and so I did. I made an appointment with a nice woman doctor. "See you later," I said to my family and drove away.

I thought I'd be safe at the gynecologist's.

The nice doctor examined me inside and out and then called me into her office. The doctor sat behind a desk. It was a pleasant room with water trickling over stones in a plug-in fountain. She needed to ask a few questions. I nodded.

"Have you had more than one sexual partner?" the doctor asked. Outside, sun was shining on the snow. This was not the question I was expecting.

"Yes," I said. Land sakes, yes.

"More than five?"

"Quite a few more," I said, as modestly as I could. I didn't want to appear to be bragging, so I added, by way of explanation, "It was the sixties."

"Have you ever had a sexually transmitted disease?" was the next question. It seemed a little nosy, but I answered truthfully.

"Yes," I said. But now I was remembering how I got it and who I gave it to, and it was Washington Square and I was young and slender and barefoot and it was 1968 all over again.

Damn, I thought.

It turned out that Medicare will pay for certain yearly exams if you have had more than five sexual partners. Who knew?

But now, instead of being safe and sound and insulated against desire (shudder), I was suddenly thinking other kinds of thoughts, having other kinds of memories. I went and bought *Guitar Town* by Steve Earle instead of listening to my better self, and I even played it indoors because when I got home the kids were out. After a bit, and despite my new relationship with time, I began to experience impatience. One song at a time was taking too long. I began to wonder if there wasn't some way I could cram all this music in at once. Oh hell.

That's called fucking.

Old Lady

I have to stop smoking. My driver's license needs renewing in 2015 and will last another ten years and I am struck by the thought that if I keep smoking a pack a day I may expire before it does. I put on my nicotine patches and hope for the best.

Now I am sitting in the window of Bread Alone while my car gets inspected at the Mobil station, which reminds me again of mortality and the worry that I may die before I'm ready. *I should get out more often,* I'm thinking now, pouring half-and-half and four tablespoons of sugar into my iced coffee. I'm still sitting in the window and I'm watching men in the rental unit of Houst & Son fiddling with engines and backing up huge tractors into tiny spaces, and one of the guys is smoking, and I calculate that my youngest grandchildren would be only fourteen if I died at seventy-seven and I want to see who they turn out to be. My oldest grandchild is twenty-five; the youngest twins will be four in February. They are all so interesting, but I don't get to live forever.

It isn't just the dying part; it's the thought of the day coming when I will have already *been* dead five, ten, two hundred years. All those centuries piling on top of me, like so many fallen trees. The fact that I will neither know nor care is of little comfort because I'm not, as yet, dead. The only cure for the fear of death is death.

If I make it to seventy-seven, the license after that will last until I'm eighty-six, but maybe by then I won't be driving anymore. I imagine my kids hiding my car keys the way my sisters and I hid our mother's car keys after six months of tolerating her driving at four miles per hour and coming to a complete stop at every light, including the green ones. We could live with that.

But then one day our mother came home saying she thought she had run over something. She didn't know what it was. She was shaking. She said "child." There were branches down from a storm, we reminded her, but she could not be comforted, no matter how many times we said that in our tiny community we would know the instant something terrible happened.

So my sisters and I whispered together in our mother's kitchen and then we snuck the car keys out of her bag and hid them in the bookcase on top of James Thurber and that was that, because Dreesen's Market delivered, and our mother never wanted to leave the house anymore anyway, but spent her days sitting in our father's old chair feeding her little dog cheese and chocolate no matter how we railed against it. "But the dog loves it," our mother said, breaking off another piece, after all she had survived eighty-plus years on cheese and chocolate herself.

All of which leads me to wonder what kind of old lady I will be. I'm already well past middle age unless I plan to live to 136, and a student recently described me as a "nice old lady with a tattoo," which startled me because I think of myself as not nice, not old, nor a lady. Didn't she see me smoking? and downing shots of tequila? Not to mention all the flirting that went on between me and that nice man to whom I took an instant liking? I don't feel like an old lady unless this is how an old lady feels.

Connective Tissue

Catherine was explaining to her boys, then aged four, about the long journey from Philadelphia, where they lived, to Woodstock. "It's made of many different legs," she said, "think of the journey as made of different legs. The New Jersey Turnpike, the New York Thruway, Route Twenty-Eight . . ."

They were on Route 6 at the time. "Is this a leg?" they asked.

"No," she said, "this is more like connective tissue." And those words struck both boys as screamingly funny. They began laughing, and for days after, one of them said to the other "connective tissue" and the insane laughter began again.

Belize

Chuck and I went with our friend Ann to Belize. It was lovely, the sea a few steps away, the skies a deep blue, the food delicious. "There are two kinds of people," Chuck said. He and I were sitting on the deck, that first day, already homesick. "There are those who count the days left of vacation, and those who count the days until they get to go home. That's us."

My room had ants on the floor, great big ones, the kind you imagine ride motorcycles and swing chains. Chuck sprayed them while I stood on my bed. His bed upstairs had biting creatures, maybe bedbugs. Every morning he woke covered with welts.

"You can sleep in my bed, if you want to," I said.

"You've been trying to get me in your bed for years, Abigail," he said, laughing.

"You wish," I said.

Machismo. Machisma.

Ocean

I've been trying to make an ocean. For some reason it never works. So I make another forest, which also doesn't work, but I don't give up on forests, so I scrape and add various blues and greens to make more trees, but it's still not to my liking. Some days are like this. I do a little halfhearted scraping, turn it over, and presto, there is the ocean, beautiful, many colors blue, deep water, no sky. I love the way this crazy shit works. When you've given up, when you least expect it, there it is.

My Will

I made a will, feeling like an adult when it was done. Pretty much everything equally divided. Catherine told me she was carrying Augie around the yard, whispering, "One day all of this will be partially yours."

Hair

Catherine's boys have fine hair that tangles in the back. I watch as she tries in vain to pull a brush through the curls. Her sons protest, wriggling and complaining. We are sitting outside the kitchen in what I laughingly refer to as the patio, full of mismatched chairs, faulty tables, and dead plants. Catherine often declares that one of the most traumatic moments in her childhood was a day when my sister Judy and I tried to get the tangles out of her hair with a bottle of Tame, failed, and, as a last resort, cut her hair. "You and Judy threw me in the shower and then you cut off *all* my hair!"

I had no good answer, just that it had to be done.

"Why didn't you brush it more often?" she may have said, or at least implied. "You wouldn't let me," I replied, or thought of replying. I smile now, as she gives up and the boys run off to ride their bikes or play with the hose, or climb the kitchen steps in order to jump off. "Watch me fly," they call now, their arms perpendicular at the sides of their bodies. "Watch, I am flying," they cry, and they zoom up and down the driveway.

Cell Phone

Sometimes Chuck's cell phone calls and I find a message consisting of him having lunch with other people or who knows what. I can hear muffled voices and silverware clinking on plates. These messages go on for so long that the lugubrious voice tells me I have seventeen seconds left of message-receiving time.

Today I get another call from Chuck. "Hello? Hello?" I yell, but all I hear are rustlings and mutterings, which means I am in his jacket or on the front seat of the car or I'm on the Number One train headed downtown when somebody heavy sits next to him. "Hello, hello," I yell again, and miraculously he picks up.

"How long have you been listening to me?" Chuck asks.

"About thirty-five years," I say.

Sixteen Again

It was fun while it lasted, and it lasted three hours and forty-five minutes, from six-forty-five until ten-thirty. That's when the restaurant closed. It wasn't a blind date because I'd seen him around, first at Yum Yum, a tiny restaurant in Woodstock, where he looked gentle and gallant, and next at an art opening, where he looked angry. I was struck by his angular face, and asked my friend Bar if she knew who he was. She nodded, saying she thought he was a sculptor. "I love the way he looks," I said. A week later he turned up in the audience of a concert Bar gave (she is a wonderful singer-songwriter), and afterward she told him she knew a woman who'd like to meet him, but that the woman was shy. "Tell her that if she doesn't call I won't eat for a week," he said, which charmed the hell out of us. He (let's call him Luther) gave Bar his number and email so I could get in touch. The telephone was more than I could handle, so I emailed. We made plans to meet the following Monday.

The best way to prepare for an evening out when you're pushing seventy is to put the blue eyeliner on before you make coffee in the morning. Eyeliner always looks best after being napped in, blinked on, and showered with, and over the span of a day achieves the smudgy look so prized by Egyptians. The same is true for blush. Put a lot of it on early, and as the day passes it may begin to look natural. I recently found out that if your face is as lined as mine it is better to use cream than powder. I had always thought it was the other way around. "Put it on the apples of your cheeks," said the pretty young woman who had also asked as tactfully as she could if I spent a lot of time in the sun.

"Every chance I get," I told her.

By six-forty-five both blush and eyeliner looked perfect. I wore a black skirt and a red velvet shirt and my best flowered Betsey Johnson tights, since my ankles are now my best feature. I showed up on time. Three young women were ahead of me in line, whispering, then one turned around and shyly declared me her favorite writer. I thanked her, we blushed, and they were shown to their table. *What a lovely way to begin an evening,* I thought. *Oh, I wish Luther had seen it,* I thought.

I had prepared myself to see Luther's face fall when we met, but he betrayed no disappointment or surprise. Hello and hello, a pleasant shaking of hands, we took a seat at the bar. He was handsome. His shoulders were like great big folded angel wings. He was tall. His face was bony and also very deeply lined, and he looked as if he made things. We ordered drinks. I had a Manhattan, he had a ginger ale. *When did you stop drinking?* I wondered, because he didn't look like a man who'd been ordering ginger ale all his life. Was I hungry? Oh yes. We moved to a table by the window overlooking the icy creek I can never remember the name of.

I think I loved him from the moment he looked at the menu, read "petit rack of lamb," and asked the waitress how big the portion was going to be. "That's just what they call the way they cut the chops," she explained, "nothing to do with size." He had the lamb, and I forget what I had. (I never forget what I have.) We talked about making things, we talked about how he began a sculpture, "with a gesture," he said, swooping his arm in the air.

We talked about what he did after the gesture part was over, and what he did was a lot like what I do with writing, figure out what it's all about by heading off in different directions, and it was all very exciting. He talked about the boring suburb where he grew up, and how in his early twenties he had become a wilderness leader. Then, when he was proficient at everything—rivers, mountains, rock climbing—"there was nothing left," he said, "but to take acid and go into the woods."

Acid scares me to death, and so do the woods. I asked if he'd ever had a bad trip. He shook his head. "The trick is to get out of the house in time," he said.

"When did you stop drinking?" I asked.

"Eight years ago," he said.

We looked out the window at the creek, the shifting patterns of dark water and thin pale ice, and the flat rocks on the bank. "I have already recorded the shape and color of those stones," he said. This reminded me of *The Bourne Identity* when Matt Damon told Franka Potente: "I can tell you the license plate numbers of all six cars outside," but I didn't say so.

Somebody bought us a round of drinks; the waitress wouldn't tell us who, they wanted to be anonymous. I thought maybe it was the nice young woman who had spoken to me earlier. "No tip unless you tell us," Luther said, but she kept her secret. I kept wanting to lean across the table and kiss him. "Hold still," I wanted to say. I haven't felt like that in twenty years. We were still talking when we realized the restaurant was closing. We split the bill, got up to leave. He introduced me to two friends still at the bar, both of whom were named John. Then we left. He peered into the back of my car and mentioned something about the dog food there. "I'd love to do this again," I said, and he said something I didn't hear because I was opening the car door.

I got home and called Bar. "I had the best time," I said. "I just love him."

I never saw him again. I emailed him after a day or two saying I hoped he'd had as good a time as I had, and asking him a quick question about something he'd said. "Who was it you said said 'Man wants but little here below but wants that little long'? Was it Oliver someone?" Of course I knew the answer.

His reply was brief. "Yes, Goldsmith, but not *but*, it's *nor*." Not another word.

Oh my god, I thought. *You're a* dick! But being seventy has its advantages. I did not spend any time wondering what I'd done wrong, or what I could or should have done differently, whether I was too old or too fat or ask too many questions. I am who I am and it has taken me a long time to get here. But part of me was sad, because I liked him, and we did have a good time. It was like an island you stumble on with a stranger, and you spend a few pleasant hours together there, but you can never find the island again. I ached a little.

But then, oh god, I suddenly remembered waiting for a glimpse of Tony Wallace as he drove up or down the hill outside our house. It was 1956, I think. I swear I could hear his car coming forty miles away, and I'd rush to the window hoping for a glimpse of his elbow sticking out the driver's side if he was driving up the hill, or a girl in the passenger seat when he was driving down. Either way I was filled with love and longing, an ache that was almost pain. Tony was tall and gentle and beautiful with sad

sad eyes. He was older than I was. He had asked me out a few times, and it was he who taught me how to French-kiss on that hill overlooking the Hudson, the smell of wisteria everywhere, but finally I was just too young. *Oh, Tony,* is all I'm thinking now.

Where are you?

Sarah's Reaction

Where does Luther live, Mom?" she asked. "I want to kill him."

Vacation in Jamaica, 2010

One morning, just in time to avoid stepping on it, I saw on the veranda outside my bedroom door what looked at first like a pale nut, or a small wooden knob off a child's toy, but which turned out on closer inspection to be a snail. It just sat there. There was no clue as to where it was going, or where it had been, it might as well have dropped from the sky. I took a shower and brushed my teeth, and when I opened the door again the snail was making its slow way under a table. I watched. Its silvery track vanished on the green veranda floor in the morning heat like the vapor trail evaporating behind a jet in the sky, although the comparison messed with my sense of time and proportion. I didn't want anyone to step on what I had begun to think of as my snail, but it was headed for safety, and I went across the street to look at the beach. I was glad it was morning. My nights are crowded with worry and fear, the old timor mortis back in action.

I sat on the stone jetty surrounded by the water, wondering if that shade of blue even has a name. Cerulean? Teal? Turquoise? Nothing covers it. Then I ached for two of my children who were going through hard times. Then I thought about hurricanes. Then I wondered if I had to decide between looking at blue or green for eternity, which would I choose? Then I wondered how to paint those clouds. Then my thoughts were of no more consequence than little sticks floating in the water. It was a sweet hour.

I went back to the house and got a cup of the most delicious coffee I've ever tasted and I sat on the back porch and a few feet away a large shiny brown cockroach was staggering through the grass, very uncockroach-like, they are ordinarily such lithe creatures. Moments later, it tipped forward headfirst into a tiny declivity, dead as a doornail.

Insecticide, I thought, and looked around for my shoes.

"What's the life expectancy of a snail?" I asked my friends, and they set to work. Some live for five years, we discovered. That's a long time to be a snail.

After breakfast, I went back to my room. My bed had been made, my clothes folded, towels hung neatly on the rack, but the snail was gone. I looked for traces, but there were none; I looked under the table, and on the legs of the table. I looked on the sides of the house and the walls of the porch. I examined the sturdy mahogany shutters. Nothing. I wondered if one of the beautiful slow-moving women who keep this place shipshape had swept it up and away. *Where does it make its home?* I wondered, then realized that it was already in its fragile residence. Which reminded me that with or without a roof over our heads, or a veranda under our feet, so are we.

Spatulas

A winter afternoon spent in bed, the arthritis in my hip hurting and me too lazy to find the Advil. Rosie sleeps with me, jamming her spine into my shoulder. Ah. Heavenly. My houseful of company has gone, bed is where I am headed. Lovely. My sister Eliza calls. How was my date? she asks. "It was wonderful," I tell her, "but he's not interested in another." Eliza knows not to ask too many questions. It took me two days to get over Luther, and it's already boring.

She is going to watch a movie but won't tell me its name because she says she likes chick flicks and is too embarrassed to tell me which ones.

"How can you be embarrassed," I say, "when you know I have watched every Transporter movie five times?" I love Jason Statham. She still refuses to tell me. We are both yawning during our conversation, a lot of yawns, like something fluid we are both bathing in, or tennis. "I am going to watch *Buffy the Vampire Slayer*," I tell her and she says maybe she will too and I say "I'm up to Spike, oh yum," and she says she meant the movie. She doesn't watch series because they would keep her up too late.

We hang up. I go upstairs to check my email (nothing) and climb into bed, but the phone rings and I rush downstairs to pick it up. It is my sister again.

"Do you know what I'm doing instead of watching a chick flick?" she asks.

"What?" I say.

"I am looking at spatulas on Amazon. There are thousands of them, and they all have hundreds of ratings," and she starts her hysterical laugh, the one I love, and she goes on, "and I'm reading every one," more laughter. "It's so hard to find a *flexible* spatula," she says, her voice rising a little, and I am laughing now and thinking actually I have a flexible one and maybe I can find one for my sister for Christmas, and she is saying, "They are all so *stiff*," and then we both collapse in hysterics.

Uh-oh

I am becoming the kind of old lady who puts her lipstick on crooked and wears too much blush—of whom when she wakes in the morning and goes downstairs to make coffee, her daughter says, "Mom, you look crazy," and it's only partly because of her hair, which sticks up in bunches like feathers. The kind of old woman who can't remember the word "pastels" speaking of the chalk you draw with and forgets where she put her bag her keys her glasses her book but can remember Steve Buscemi's name and two of his movies: *Con Air* and *Fargo*.

Names I Forget

Robert Duvall
Gene Hackman
Julia Stiles (I always want to call her Clementine)
Bill Paxton
Someone else I can't remember
Roy Orbison

Late Fall

Late fall, and the color is gone. This is the season of bare trees, the kinds of trees my sister Judy describes as looking as if they died of fright. A perfect description. Judy should be a writer, I nag her all the time. "If you're not going to use it, I am," I say, but I'm careful to give credit.

The leaves this year were glorious yellows and reds and browns, but a few along Tinker Street (and one you could see only from Cumberland Farms) were a deep shade of rose. Rose! You had to gasp. But except for those moments of painfully beautiful color, I haven't felt like shouting, can't think of anything to write or paint (I don't know how to do autumn), and nothing more has occurred to me recently about failure, except that it's failure.

But when it gets dark, I'm off the hook. The day is officially rolled up and put away. I'm free to watch movies or stare at the wall, no longer holding myself accountable for what I might or might not have gotten done because the time for getting something done is over until tomorrow.

My chair is worn and comfortable, my dog Rosie is lying on the pillow behind my back, like a warm shawl. All three dogs are snoring in different registers, the two clocks tick out of sync, and I am simply enjoying being in this room alive. My body thrums with pleasure. Everything I look at I love. Just as I'm wondering if there are any cement nails lying around so I can hammer this old wooden wheel into the mortar, it hits me that these bricks are going to outlast me. Ditto the wooden wheel. This room, and almost everything in it, it's all going to be here after I die. The pleasure leaves my body. I feel a marked detachment from my surroundings, a cooling of affection for these objects. I am experiencing my own absence, and the room without me in it is just any old room, its details of no consequence. I get one of those awful moments when I feel nothing at all.

Then thank god Harry farts one of his room-clearing farts and I have to put the scarf over my nose and I get up and find *The Bourne Identity* and stick it in the DVD player and the unfeeling retreats, but doesn't disappear. Once you've felt this, you can't unfeel it. Once the carnal knowledge of your own death has jumped you, your innocent days are over. You can't put the shit back in the pig.

Remains

I have decided that when I'm dead I'd like my body in the woods under a light coating of leaves. That being against the law, maybe I will go for cremation. I ask Chuck what he wants done with his remains.

"Remains?" says Chuck. "Do there have to be remains? Can't I just vanish? Be no more?"

I tell him I'm sorry but yes, he has to have remains.

"Either I'm too young to be thinking about this," he says, "or I have to figure out a way of offing myself that will leave no remains. I could get in the shower with a chain saw," he says, "and limit the cleanup."

I don't say anything. "Or I believe some sort of explosive device might do the trick," he says, but I point out there will be remains anyway.

"It's better than being carried away in a zippered black bag and then burned," he says. This is uncomfortably real. I'm just poking at death with a long stick to see what happens.

Eggs

This morning, I woke up, let the dogs out, made the coffee, and put the fire on in the fireplace. I cover myself in my ratty old knitted blanket and I'm just sitting here on this dark morning and the clouds are gray and darker gray and I think, *God, gray, how many grays there are!* So now I'm thinking black stems and gorgeous white flowers and a dark gray sky and a big pale moon? Or gray stems and black sky? Blue stems or mix green with black stems or what, I can't decide; the only things that stay the same are the gorgeous white flowers almost like midnight moths or butterflies, luscious like the fat juiciness of lichee fruit, or gardenias, and I know I can make these and I jump up and first write this down lest it get lost and now I'm heading out back to look at my eleven-by-fourteen piece of glass until it tells me what it wants to be.

Later, on a piece of plate glass thirty by fourteen that used to be a shelf in the Golden Notebook's children's section, I make a row of fried eggs with gorgeous yellow yolks.

It is now three days later and I have made dozens of eggs. I can't stop. I want the world to see them. The eggs are turning me into an entrepreneur. I don't want to sell them, but I am thinking of ways I could.

One Difference

One difference between painting and writing is that when I'm done with a painting and I love it, I don't care what anyone else thinks. If someone comes into my studio and says only "My, you've been busy," I don't take it out on my paintings. I simply never ask this person over for coffee again.

No Stiff Necks

Here's what I love about dogs. They aren't careful not to disturb you. They don't overthink. They jump on the bed or the sofa or the chair and plop down. They come and they go. I'm not sure they love me exactly, but they count on me because I am a source of heat and food and pleasure and affection. If one of them is lying next to me and suddenly prefers the sofa, I don't take it personally. Dogs don't wake up on the wrong side of the bed. There is no wrong side of the bed for a dog.

I used to lie in a lover's arms getting a stiff neck, or needing to scratch my nose, or losing all sensation in my arm, unwilling to move lest the man find out I wasn't comfortable in his embrace. I spent hours hyperventilating in the arms of my soon to be second husband, feeling claustrophobic and terrified, yet unable to free myself lest I disturb his sleep. Would Snow White have rested all eight pounds of her head on any part of the prince? I doubt it, and I never did either. Sarah says that is why elderly women have such prominent cords in their necks.

Deaf

Harry is going deaf. Still, he lifts his head to monitor a scent drifting through the closed but leaky windows and up he gets, creakily, and off he limps to the back door to strut what remains of his stuff. He has never learned to negotiate the dog door flap, so I rise, also creakily, to let him out. The other two, Rosie and Carolina, who were awakened by Harry, have already zoomed past us into the yard, noses to the ground. Rosie's hearing even at eleven is fine. She can hear me open my eyes. Carolina is all about her nose. I love their enthusiasm. Sometimes I see Rosie rolling on her back in the ice-crusted snow, all four legs pawing at air, having a ball. Carolina can howl for hours, which is admirable, but a mixed blessing. I think it's because she can't complete the circuit. Whatever varmint traipsed through the yard last night passed over the underground electrical fence that keeps Carolina in the yard. So she has to keep going back over old ground, running in circles. No payoff.

My hearing is no longer keen either. A goldfish coming to the surface of the bowl blowing bubbles used to keep me awake. Now I watch American movies with the subtitles on; I cup my hand behind my ear when sitting with a murmurer, and cup my hands behind both ears in a restaurant, but the loss has been incremental so it's no big deal. The curious thing is that, as if to make up for what I'm missing, I am now hearing things that aren't happening: voices, conversations, messages left on my answering machine that aren't there when I run downstairs to

106

retrieve them. Maybe what I am hearing are ghosts of conversations. Today from the bottom of my pocketbook while I was unpacking groceries I heard a man's voice saying something that sounded pleasant but when I dug to the bottom, my cell phone was off. No message. No record of a new call. I can accept this. Stranger things have happened. I tell Catherine, who has come for tea. She is alarmed. "Mom," she says. "Maybe you should have a CT scan."

"Don't worry," I say, putting a PG Tips tea bag in her mug. "It's been happening for years. It's not getting worse. Besides, I'm not hearing voices, I'm *overhearing* them. I just don't know what they are saying."

I'm also losing my memory. Great chunks are falling away, like cliffs into the sea. I never had a good memory, so the loss of a name or a month or what I am doing in the kitchen (living room bedroom dining room yard) is familiar. Telephone conversations after nine at night seem to be lost forever. What I read last week, vanished. What I read yesterday, pretty much ditto. But this evening I asked my grandson Joe what he did today and he told me. Four minutes later I asked him what he did today. Joe is twenty-six, and kind, and he began to tell me again. "Oh god," I said, interrupting him, "I'm so sorry. I think my brain is erasing itself."

"I forget all the time," said Joe, "I forgot . . ." and then he told me something he forgot, which I've forgotten.

He is very nice to have around. He has been living with me about a month now, and his brother Sam visits often. They are in their twenties figuring out their lives. I keep wanting to say, "Forget career, forget the future, forget existential worries, just get yourselves a couple of dogs, and everything will be all right."

The way I remember how long they've been here is by the number of meals I have actually cooked. I still have a good memory for food. Pork tenderloin, lamb stew, chicken soup with dumplings, roast chicken with carrots and onions, pasta with capers and tuna and lemon juice and olive oil and other things I forget. Baked Indian pudding, made with sorghum from Kentucky.

But that's as far back as my memory goes.

I have been meaning to write more about losing my mind, but instead I keep falling asleep. Anyway, besides what I'm forgetting, and besides what I can no longer hear, I'm recalling all kinds of unnecessary things like going to Sardi's when I was fourteen with Tony Wallace and his family and seeing an actress named Betsy Palmer at a neighboring table. I was wearing a scoop-neck black velvet blouse belonging to my mother, and it didn't fit. I ordered pheasant under glass because I'd never heard of it. Why do I remember this? But I do, vividly. Now it turns out I might have gone to Sardi's with Barry Burcaw and his family. I spoke to Barry recently, and he remembered an evening we spent there with his parents. We were both of us children. Back then, according to him, I was someone I don't recognize or remember: pretty, charming, unattainable, perfect crush material for a boy in the seventh grade. A couple of years later my family moved away and the future shifted.

Go Figure

Catherine and Tim and the boys moved from Philadelphia to Woodstock. They bought an eccentric old farmhouse with five acres of woods. Chuck and I went to their closing and then took them out to dinner at the Red Onion. "Why is it you're here for all my family's momentous occasions?" Tim asked Chuck, but I don't think he needed an answer.

It took Tim a long time to get past Chuck and Catherine's affair. He and Catherine had been going out, but then Tim moved to Philadelphia and the two of them were taking a break. But it was a break, not a breakup, and Tim was angry with Chuck. Now we have Thanksgivings together, and birthdays, and Tuesday night movies at my house.

Right after Catherine moved, Chuck moved too. He found a house in Woodstock with a nice yard and a big studio.

My Eyes

My peripheral vision was tested recently. One eye at a time stared into inky blackness, and I had to hit a buzzer whenever I saw tiny flashes of light, like stars disappearing and reappearing in another, more distant part of the cosmos. Both eyes did fine. Then the doctor stared into my eyeballs, seeing nothing out of the ordinary; my left eye has the beginnings of a cataract, no big deal, although it made me feel old. The day before, while driving on the Mass Pike to see my daughter Jennifer, I noticed that if I looked at the right red taillight of the car in front of me, I couldn't see the left. It was alarming. Blinking didn't help. Rubbing my eyes didn't help. Willpower didn't help. I'd never lost control of a body part before except during childbirth. It kept amazing me that I couldn't fix it. The situation lasted about twenty minutes. When I got to the Prudential Center exit, I called Chuck and told him. "Something sort of interesting happened to me," I began, then described it. He called me back twenty minutes later. "Is one side weaker than the other? Is half of your face sagging? Do you feel tingling?" No on all counts. "Then I think you're okay for now," he said. "But call your doctor."

I didn't tell anyone else because I was on a mission of mercy to Jamaica Plain to help Jen with her five-year-old twins, both of whom have asthma. This time it was Violet. She had been coughing and wheezing, and Jen was afraid she would wind up in the ER again. I would take care of Ralphie, he of the room-brightening but seldom seen smile. I looked forward to hours of Lego. The next morning I finally told Jen about my episode of partial blindness and she insisted I call my doctor and my doctor insisted I go to the ER, where they found no sign of a stroke, thank god. Not knowing what else to do with me, they sent me to an ophthalmologist, who thought perhaps I had had an ocular migraine. The doctors were puzzled but not overly concerned. They prescribed an aspirin a day, which I now regard as a sacrament.

Two nights later I woke up in Jen's bed (she slept with the twins) experiencing an electric shock, as if I had just stuck my finger in a light socket. My skin tingled for minutes. *Oh my god*, I thought, *I'm shorting out!* The next morning I wasted no time telling Jen, who immediately looked this phenomenon up and discovered it not uncommon, that our bodies often give us electric shocks, sometimes to the tune of dozens a day. It's not dangerous. We are electric after all, which is hard to remember because inside we are so wet. I breathe in and out, thinking we are really machines, fleshy machines, oxygen in, carbon dioxide out. Why am I not aware of this more often, us being such miracles, so well put together? Alive!

An Entry from Jennifer's Blog

Last Sunday was Father's Day. Catherine and I were catching up on the phone this morning and I mentioned that Ralphie has been talking a lot about wishing he had a dad. Catherine said, without missing a beat, "Well, Augie and Freddy wish they had a unicorn."

My Old Dog

Harry is beginning to have trouble climbing the stairs, and spends some nights on two pillows by the pellet stove in the living room. He is still having a good time, he loves to eat, he loves his belly rubbed. *Will you make it through this winter, my old friend?* I wonder, and refuse to believe the voice that says no.

Then he develops a deadly sounding cough, and at my own checkup the doctor hears something in my heart that wasn't there last year and my blood pressure is no longer 120 over 70, far from it. The doctor can hear the murmur only when I'm sitting up, which might be good, since I love to nap. Still, I realize, making my echocardiogram appointment, I'm mortal.

When I take Harry to the vet the doctor says he has a "pretty significant heart murmur," which worries me, and he has his own appointment for an echocardiogram. He's an old dog. So am I. This morning I am waiting to hear our results. There are two clocks ticking but not in unison. Tick tick tock tock. I am sitting in my big chair and Harry is asleep on his cushion.

It turns out Harry and I are both if not exactly fine, not at death's door either. Harry has to take a diuretic, and my doctor pronounces my condition "nothing earth-shattering." The name is horrible: "mild mitral regurgitation," but I can live with it.

I still have to quit smoking. I impulsively dropped what I hoped would be my last cigarette into a cup of cold coffee and applied a nicotine patch to my shoulder. Then I sat there in my chair. My daughter Jennifer called and we discussed birthday presents for the twins (trucks, dresses, and Legos); I talked to my son, Ralph, about singing lessons for his daughter Justine's birthday; I drank some orange juice and ate some carrots and watched a vampire movie and then took myself off to bed early. It wasn't even nine o'clock.

I settled in bed with my three pillows and my three dogs, the curtains pulled, door closed, fan on, lights off, everything the way I like it, but this time my heart was pounding in my throat. Out of the blue came a fact: this body of mine, the one in pink pajamas, the one hanging on to her pillow for dear life, these pleasant accommodations in which I have made my home for seventy years, it's going to die. It will die, and the rest of me, homeless, will disappear into thin air. I could actually *hear* my heart now, pounding.

But hard on the heels of this came a worse bit of news. My beautiful children, now in the middle of their lives, are going to grow old and they are going to die too. If I could somehow come back in thirty years, I might not even recognize them—white-haired, frail, they would be elderly strangers. When that thought struck, I felt an awful meaninglessness, and then nothing, and that absence of feeling was the worst thing I've ever felt.

The next morning the dogs woke up early, and we headed downstairs, all except Harry, who slept in. I opened the door, and Rosie and Carolina raced into the dark, noses to the ground, tails waving in the air, tracking whatever creatures had criss-crossed our yard during the night. When Harry finally got up, he barked at the top of the stairs, calling for me to wait for him at the bottom before he made his cautious way down. Before he went out, he checked everybody's bowl. Harry's an optimist.

I love this old dog. Off he ambled into the yard, tail held high, head held high. Peeing on everything perpendicular.

Cold and gray. A long day ahead, and I don't know how to fill it. I'm not painting, I'm not writing. I'm depressed. Morbid. I measured the water and the coffee and plugged the pot in and worried about the day stretching ahead.

Then I had a bit of luck. Yesterday I discovered a bowl of plums in the icebox that had sat there forgotten for a month, and I took the bowl into the backyard and tossed the plums one by one onto the icy grass near the woods where I've seen deer. A dozen dusky purple plums, past their prime: an offering. And this morning when I went out to look the frozen grass was bare, and I was filled with a joy I can't get to the bottom of.

Years Later I Hear of a Proposal

This morning Catherine tells me that the day after Rich's accident, Chuck asked her to marry him. "I don't know what he was thinking," she says. Later that afternoon Chuck tells me that the day after Rich's accident he asked Catherine to marry him. "She said no," he tells me.

I don't know what to do with this information. It's like being served a meal you didn't order and couldn't possibly eat, and all I want to do is send it back to the kitchen.

Why on earth are they telling me this on the same day? When I ask them later, they are both surprised.

Chronology

I hate chronological order. Not only do I have zero memory for what happened when in what year, but it's so *boring*. This comes out of me with the kind of vehemence that requires a closer look, so I scribble on the back of a napkin while waiting for friends to show up at Cucina and it doesn't take long to figure it out. The thought that this happened and then this happened and then this and this and this, the relentless march of event and emotion tied together simply because day follows day and turns into week following week becoming months and years reinforces the fact that the only logical ending for chronological order is death.

Hep C

Chuck had an appointment with his liver doctor. He sees her every six months to check on the progress of the disease. We know he has stage four cirrhosis, but so far he is holding his own. He didn't call when he got home, which he usually does. I called him.

"What did she say?" I asked. I'm not shy about this.

"She says I have three years." Chuck laughs.

"*What?*" I say.

"Just kidding," he says and changes the subject.

I call Catherine.

"Will you please ask him what's going on?"

But he's already called Catherine and told her it was all a joke.

Rather Die

Chuck calls to say he's decided to become a geriatric nurse so he can take care of me in what he refers to as my rapidly approaching old age.

"And this friendship will finally be consummated," he says, which I guess is nice of him, but all I can visualize are bedpans and gruel.

"I think I'd rather die," I say.

Hospice

I decided to take the training for becoming a hospice volunteer. I need something to make me feel useful. I told Chuck.

"Just in time," said Chuck.

"Ha ha ha," I said.

I want to make Death a member of my family. I don't want it to arrive as a stranger.

The Information

During the last seventy-two hours of a person's life, there will be a discoloration of toes and kneecaps, a marked coolness of hands and feet. There will be mental confusion, and a mottling of the skin, which will start at the feet and progress up the legs. When mottling reaches the upper thighs, death is imminent. Two minutes after the heart stops beating, the person is still aware. This is what happens during the course of a natural death, an easy death.

There are other scenarios—a bleed-out, for instance. If there is bleeding from the mouth and nose, we are to cover the blood with dark towels. There will be a large quantity of blood, and we want to spare the family the sight of it. If there is an internal bleed-out from a tumor in the esophagus, say, or a tumor in the lungs, there will be no visible blood. The instructor says if this is happening, we hold the patient's hand and wait. Death will take only a few minutes.

Hold the patient's hand and wait. The simplicity is so moving. It strikes me that the physical details of the dying body are as intimate and predictable as those of the body making love.

The Training

Twelve of us sit around a big table. We are given a bad diagnosis and twelve squares of paper. On the first three we are to write the names of three people dear to us. On the next three, things we cherish. On the next three, stuff we enjoy. On the last three, things about ourselves we value. We spread the squares in front of us neatly on the table. Then we are given six months to live.

The instructor describes the disease's progress month by month. As each month passes, and our condition worsens, we must tear up two pieces of paper. The instructor comes around the table and collects the torn pieces in a shopping bag. By the end of the six months, when we are too weak to sit up, too weak to eat, when we have lost so much weight that our clothes hang off our bodies, we each have two pieces of paper left. The instructor comes around the table and from us she takes one of the last two pieces, tears it up, and drops it in her shopping bag. The room is quiet. We are each left with one piece of paper. Then she tells us to tear that up too.

Tirade Against "He Passed Away"

You never hear it said, "He is passing away." It is always a fait accompli. "He passed." How I hate it. As if the body had nothing to do with it, as if the body hadn't even been around at the time but off playing Scrabble somewhere, or having a drink while the tenant moved out. Dying is the body's call, the shutting down of services is the body's last bit of business. Give credit where credit is due. Honor the process. Consider the simple dignity of "She is dying." Or "He died."

It *is* interesting to think of it as a verb.

III

THE WILDERNESS OF
NOT KNOWING

Death of Dogs

Of the three dogs I once had, only my old hound Carolina survives. She runs around the yard early in the morning, following scents in circles, occasionally lifting her head to howl. When I bring her in, she looks relieved and sleeps for the rest of the day.

Harry, my elderly beagle, died first and peacefully on his pillow in front of the fire. My grandson Joe was living here then. Harry was failing, and Joe volunteered to sleep on the couch, ready to alert me if anything changed. When Harry's breathing stopped being labored and became intermittent, Joe woke me. It was six in the morning. We sat down on the floor by Harry's pillow. "You're a good dog, Harry," we said, stroking his fur. He died half an hour later. His body relaxed, and when his tongue lolled from his mouth it was gray. Gray.

Joe buried him in the garden, and planted a weeping cherry, which is weeping again this spring.

Then Rosie, my favorite (I admit I had a favorite), died in my arms last November. I knew she was dying, I'd known it all day, and I carried her upstairs to bed, where we lay all afternoon, and into the night. Occasionally she turned her head to look at me. "I'm right here," I said. Now and then she would lap a little water from a bowl. She tried desperately to get out of bed when she had to pee, but collapsed on the rug. I picked her up, and we lay together until quarter to ten, when she let out a dreadfully human groan, and I held her and held her and when it was done I was old.

Rosie

I think of Rosie all the time. She is buried where I can see her grave from the kitchen window, a slab of bluestone covered with pebbles and flowers and a little plastic angel my friend Roland brought over. I miss her. *Hello, my girl,* I say, but I don't think she hears. *Hello, Rosie,* I say anyway, *Hello my darling.* Joe planted a rose tree for her, and it has started to bloom.

Years ago Jen took a picture of my Rosie, and gave it to me framed for a birthday. Her muzzle was already going white, but she is looking up at me with that look only she had, the look that meant "You are mine and we both know it." I remember thinking one day this would be all I'd have left of her. I keep the photo in my kitchen window, and looking at it brings Rosie right back, although loss comes along for the ride.

She used to sleep on the cushion behind my back in the big red chair, like a warm living shawl. When another dog walked by, she growled. After she died, I stopped sitting there and moved the chair to another room.

I like to remember her last meal was roast beef from Woodstock Meats. Sarah had been staying with me, and she brought it home for Rosie. She ate it all, from Sarah's hand.

Alcohol

Cooper is one of my two new dogs. My daughter Jen found him for me. He is a bluetick hound from Kentucky. He is dignified and solitary. A friend said he looks as though he might have been a historian in another life.

Cooper wakes up at 5:30 A.M., you can set your watch by him. He makes moaning sounds that develop into howls, then Carolina and Daphne (my newest hound rescue) jump off the bed, and all three mill around my bedroom barking until I get up. I brush my teeth, make my coffee, feed the dogs, and let them out. They crowd the dog door, scrambling and shouldering each other out of the way, then run noisily into the yard.

Until two weeks ago I then would find cigarettes and disappear into my studio with a beer. Not just any beer, a beauty of a Belgian beer, a full meal of a beer, Rochefort 10. I told myself drinking early stimulates my imagination, frees me from care, and spreads my drinking throughout the day, thereby lessening its effect. I would then drink another beer and continue to paint. Alcohol, I reasoned, deadens pain, the dread I felt most of the time. By ten in the morning I would be sloshed.

I thought nobody knew how much and how early I was drinking, but the cumulative effect began to be obvious. When Chuck and I went to Cucina, me already half in the bag, I'd have a Manhattan or two. I told myself it dulled my worry, or else it enhanced what I didn't allow myself to feel, whichever was appropriate to the moment. When I ordered a third, Chuck frowned.

"I know it's a slippery slope," I said, taking a swallow.

"It's not a slippery slope for you, Abigail," he said, nursing the Knob Creek he shouldn't have been drinking. "It's a waterslide."

"And you?" I said. "Your liver is shot to hell."

Chuck shrugged.

Then my son, Ralph, visiting for the weekend, sat me down. He is very gentle, but he talks straight. "Ma," he said, "I have to be honest with you. You need to think about what you're doing." Beer bottles were everywhere, by the sides of chairs, next to the sofa, under the sofa, next to the telephone, half a dozen in my studio, several on my desk, and the recycling bin was full. "Drinking isn't reality," he said. "Reality is better than nonreality. Even scary reality."

But I had my reasons.

"I have one more beer," I finally said, "and I'm going to drink it." I did, and that, I thought, was that. Done.

Daphne

Daphne, my newest dog, ducks under the covers and makes her way to the end of the bed. She places her forelegs over my ankles, then lays her head on my feet. She licks me for a while, which provides a surprisingly pleasant sensation, then falls asleep. From time to time I can feel her delicate swallow, now and then her legs pump and I know she's running after something in the backyard, sometimes she just moves her jaws with none of the muffled barking the other two dogs do (a hilarious sound, barking with mouth closed) but I'm pretty sure Daphne is dreaming of eating. Or chewing. The lawn is littered with items stolen from everywhere—rolls of paper towels mutilated and scattered, loaves of raisin bread, only the wrappers remaining; an entire box of black-and-white cookies; the brisket I had wrapped up for my daughter, the only part of which remained (when I turned my back for two minutes) was the tinfoil. Daphne has stolen all the books from the bottom shelf (writers whose last names begin with "E"). I have found Jeffrey Eugenides, George Eliot, Alice Thomas Ellis, Clyde Edgerton, Deborah Eisenberg, all lying on the lawn with their bindings chewed. The red comforter has been reduced to fluff, the green coverlet is now lace. I don't dare put anything pretty on my bed lest it be turned to ribbons, so I sleep under rags. I don't care. I love her. Yesterday I caught her just in time scooting through the dog door with my daughter Catherine's baseball cap, the one with the bronze wig attached. Catherine has cancer. She has other wigs, but this one's her favorite.

Finding Out

She found a lump in her breast, summer of 2011. She went to the doctor, and had a biopsy. A week went by. The results were supposed to come on Monday, and Catherine drove to my house to wait for the call. When her phone rang she stiffened. "It's them," she said, and listened for a moment before she turned away, her shoulders shaking. "Is this a death sentence?" I heard her whisper, weeping. I put my arms around her. Catherine makes no sound when she weeps, but her body heaves and trembles. "It will be all right," I told her. "It will be all right." But my body was ice-cold.

I called her sisters and her brother, who had one question. *Will she be all right?*

"Of course," I think I said. "Of course she will."

Then I called Chuck. "It's cancer," I told him.

"God, no," he said.

"I'm terrified," I said.

Triple Negative

Catherine's cancer is triple negative, which means there is no standard treatment. "I'm going to try to look on this as an adventure, Mom," she said, and my heart broke for her innocence and courage.

"Triple negative" means that Catherine's cancer cells don't have receptors for estrogen, progesterone, or HER2. As a result, her cancer cells don't respond to therapies that block estrogen, progesterone, or HER2. There is no protocol. Furthermore, because there are no effective treatments, this cancer is extremely aggressive. "Likely to recur," said a hospital pamphlet in a doctor's waiting room. Afraid that Catherine might read this terrifying phrase (why could they not have said "*more* likely to recur"?), I stuffed the damn thing in my bag to toss, but it sticks with me.

Help

J ennifer came down, and Ralph, and Sarah. Everyone helped. The community helped. The cancer support center in Kingston helped. My friend Amy was generous with her advice, and brought food to the hospital while we waited for Catherine's turn. Friends brought suppers to the little family.

On the corridor wall of the main hospital, Catherine and I walked past a photograph of my father, who had once been the head of Memorial Sloan Kettering. We always stopped there for a minute, both of us wishing he were still here. He would say something gentle.

Treatment

The waiting room at Evelyn H. Lauder Center is cheerful and bright, one side all windows. There are comfortable chairs, tables filled with magazines. The waiting room was filled, but we found seats by the window. Around us were women young and old, wealthy and not, some with family accompanying them, some alone. When Catherine's name was called, I waited for everyone to lift their heads in amazement as this beautiful young woman rose from her chair. Nobody even glanced up. Who could help but notice that this daughter of mine was the loveliest woman they had ever seen? I was angry. Why didn't every head turn in sorrow?

The oncologist recommended a lumpectomy. The following week, after surgery, the surgeon came to tell us the margins were clear. They had gotten all of it out. No lymph node involvement. Good news.

Therapies

I drove Catherine into the city once a week for chemo. We stayed at my sister Judy's apartment the night before. Judy made us laugh, gave Catherine presents, baked popovers for us in the mornings. She was so funny and so kind. She insisted on giving us her bed. Catherine and I never sleep under the sheets but wrap ourselves in comforters, and Catherine always spills her tea and I drink coffee without using a saucer, and Judy, a very tidy soul, would give us a withering look, then announce, "Barbarians!" It was always funny. We looked forward to these weekly visits.

Tim was working in the city and often met us in the waiting room. The days were long, and Catherine scarfed up all the good trashy magazines and we settled ourselves near the windows. "I don't know who any of these people are," I said to her, looking at the covers of six *People* magazines. "I don't either, Mom," she said, but we read them anyway.

The chemo rooms were airy and private. Catherine was getting infusions of several drugs. The nurses were kind and expert with the needle, and Catherine usually fell asleep, her hands clutching the pillow on her lap. After chemo, if she was up to it, we shopped at the Whole Foods on Columbus Avenue, stocking up on cookies. Driving home, Catherine slept on a pillow against the window, wrapped in blankets.

Then, three months into chemo, another tumor appeared. Catherine was immediately scheduled for a mastectomy. I called

Chuck. "Another tumor," I said. "How can this be happening? How can it have grown right in the middle of chemo?"

"But that's what this cancer is," he said quietly. "That's what it does."

Chuck spoke gently, but he was matter-of-fact. I was still afraid, but the shock was gone.

Radiation

After she healed from the mastectomy, Catherine opted for six weeks of radiation, five days a week. We used the radiology lab at Benedictine Hospital, fifteen minutes away. No more trips to New York.

"I miss Judy," Catherine said.

Tim & Catherine

Tim puts his arms around Catherine as if to keep her safe forever. The two of them in one another's arms are like a point on the map, a location in time, a destination. Jennifer took a picture of this embrace, and I love to look at it.

Unsympathetic

Not long after Catherine's diagnosis, my grandson Joe is here, nursing a broken heart. He is the oldest of Sarah's five kids. Usually I am a good listener. Usually I am sympathetic to a broken heart. I love this young man, and he is clearly bewildered, even stunned by the pain. We are sitting outside on the uncomfortable wire chairs I bought years ago, and he tells us his girlfriend left him. Now she won't answer his calls. She gives no explanation for the breakup. He looks to me for advice, for reassurance, for sympathy. I look back at him with god knows what expression on my face. There is a brief silence.

"It's not cancer," I say.

"Mom," says Catherine later. She is shocked. "That was really harsh."

I don't care. I have no sympathy for ordinary grief.

Mice

Catherine comes over on Tuesdays. Today she arrived carrying a wire basket filled with soft blankets, and a sheaf of papers the top of which turned out to be instructions for feeding abandoned tiny creatures. "I have something to show you," she said, her cheeks flushed with excitement. Chuck was here and she sat between us and we watched as she carefully unwrapped the blanket, revealing in its depths the smallest live creature with four legs I ever saw: a baby mouse, no bigger than the first two joints of my little finger. Her cat Carlos had brought it in injured, two puncture wounds in its neck, but alive. Catherine is feeding him/her ("I wish I knew which," she says) with a formula she bought for abandoned kittens. She uses one of the syringes (minus the needle) she keeps to inject her diabetic cat, older than dirt, who spends most of his life asleep on the kitchen table under a vase of flowers, his scruffy back sprinkled with fallen petals.

The mouse's eyes are still closed. Its paws and nose are pink, the rest of him is a soft gray. "Look!" she says, holding the little thing in the palm of her hand, stroking its back very softly.

The mouse died half an hour later.

"I'm glad it died while I was holding it," Catherine says, tears in her eyes.

"I'm sorry," says Chuck, his arm around her shoulder.

"You did everything you could," I say, putting my hand on hers. "It was just too small to survive without its mother."

Then we all fall silent. I wish I hadn't spoken. I hope Catherine isn't thinking about what I am suddenly thinking about: her boys.

Tree

We had a hurricane. I went outside in the screaming wind and discovered, on the north side of the house, a tree leaning over at a forty-five-degree angle, its enormous root-ball cracking the surface of the ground, snarled roots dangling, and nothing to be done. A perfect example of inevitable.

Worries

When I worry about Catherine I call Chuck and he says something considered and thoughtful, which is how I know he is worried too. When I am worried about Chuck I call Catherine, and she is silent, which is how I know she is worried too. We function, at least for me, as a family. I count on Chuck the way I would on her father. Chuck cares for her in his own way too, but the role of parent suits him and helps me. Odd, after all we have been through. I don't know that we would have been as close as we are now without the breakage, the damage done. We have built something sturdy out of the wreckage.

A Dream

I looked down and there was a little bell, and I could see the silver clapper beating inside and realized, *Oh, this is my heart, what's it doing outside my body? And why is it transparent? Can everyone see?* I was nervous but kept on dreaming. Because what the hell.

Another Date

I took Augie out to Cucina the other night, as I had taken Fred the month before. "I've got to get ready, Mom," he said to Catherine hours before our date, and proceeded to dress himself. He chose a blue and white striped shirt, khaki pants, and matching socks. He wore a small snap-on necktie Catherine had bought because it reminded her of the ties her father wore.

Augie is six years old. We sat down, put our napkins in our laps, and he blew out the candle on the table. Usually I admonish him, but tonight was special. I lit the candle again, and said, "Blow it out and make a wish." He did.

"I guess it won't not come true if I tell you," he said.

"What did you wish for?" I asked.

"I wished Mommy's cancer would go away."

I wish that all the time.

I lit the candle again. He made another wish and blew it out.

"I wish for a happy family life," he said, this child of six.

Me too.

I lit the candle again. "Here's my *ultimate* wish," he said, gathering himself up to blow again. "I wish for a . . ." and then he named an action figure I can't remember the name of. He had two cherry sodas and the shrimp pasta. He didn't like the tails so he pulled them all off and placed them on the edge of my plate. I ate them. "They are very good," I told him, "thank you."

"I don't like them," he said, pulling off another and tossing it my way.

Both boys were here yesterday. We found thousands of tiny inch-high maples hiding in the grass.

"Good-bye, you little seedlings," I called to the boys when they left. Augie's voice came from the car. "Good-bye, big flower," he called.

Awful Days

What are these awful days? Days full of phone calls I don't return or even pick up; people I ought to call because of recent deaths; party invitations to which I don't even respond. I am rude and thoughtless. I can't rouse myself longer than half an hour before I again climb the stairs with the dogs for another long nap under the covers, shades drawn, fan on for white noise, telephone tucked where I can't hear it. But if this lasts too long, Jennifer alerts Catherine, and Catherine calls Chuck, and someone comes over to see if I'm okay. "Your daughters are worried about you," says Chuck this morning. "I came to see if you were dead."

Beautiful

Catherine is beautiful. Six weeks of radiation are over now, and her hair is growing in like duckling down, with waves and cowlicks; the color is a pale fawn. "You look like Ingrid Bergman in that movie," I tell her. She gives me a patient look. "I absolutely love your hair."

"You say that all the time, Mom," she says, "but this just isn't me."

Before treatment, her hair was longer and bleached blond, often with pink streaks running through it. To me she looks more like who she is now, or who she is becoming, but since there's no way to explain that to myself, I can't explain it to her.

Anger

I'm not a good cancer patient, Mom," says Catherine. "I'm not having any fun." She looks at books written by cancer survivors who detail how their lives changed—new foods to explore, a fresh outlook, appreciating life in the moment. "There is no book about how cancer sucks," she says.

But she has always had a rich appreciation for life. Most of the pictures my daughter Jennifer has taken of Catherine show her bending down to examine something in the grass. Catherine loves tiny live things; she loves fossils, flowers, bones, stones. There is a collection of river stones on her front porch, and bones of various kinds. Ralph gave her one of his most treasured possessions: a raven skull. She displays it in her office, which also contains shelves and shelves of things she has collected off the face of the earth. I bought her a trilobite in Colorado, 400 million years old. It gave us both the shivers when we held it in our hands. "Did you know, Mom," she said, "that our bodies are made out of stars? Stars and dinosaurs and grass, everything is in us. We're all part of the Big Bang. Don't you love that?"

I love her.

Anger?

Chuck and I are having breakfast at Oriole 9. "It makes me furious," I tell him, "all these people writing about how good cancer was for them, how they developed a fresh outlook on everything, how cancer changed their lives for the better. All so self-congratulatory." I'm talking through my hat, really, having read only *about* this kind of book, not the books themselves.

"I'm so angry," I say, "that all this shit makes Catherine feel inferior."

Chuck looks at me. "You might not be angry at them," he says, "you might be angry that Catherine *got* cancer."

This is a wonderfully provocative remark.

"Thank you," I say, "this gives me something to think about."

But I'm not sure it's true.

Anger is a luxury. Anger wants answers, retribution, reasons, something that makes sense. Anger wants a story, stories help us make sense out of everything. But while we scramble to help those who need it, who has time for anger? Who has time to make sense out of anything? There is only what is. Anger is a distraction. Anger removes me from grief, and the opportunity to be helpful.

Am I angry? No. Catherine is alive.

Dread

I have no use for the future and it has little use for me. I exist in the present. But I live in dread, whose roots are in the future. Dread owes its very existence to the future.

"What can come?" my grandson Sam asked, when he was very young, after his mother had warned him not to go into the woods after dark. What can come? This was a brilliant question. *Can* is scarier than *will*. What *will* come limits itself. What *can* come has no boundaries. Our family has repeated this question for years, laughing.

Dread can be all-purpose, or it can roost on a specific branch. I know my daughter is cancer-free now, at this moment, and that this moment is it.

But I admit dread has taken up residence. My daughter has been free of cancer for a year, but I'm still afraid of what can come.

The Backdrop

All of this—life, death, fear, dread, worry—is not going on in a vacuum, no matter how it sometimes feels. We live in a village with a village green and two bookstores; good coffee, nice people, crowded weekends. This is the Catskills, and I am surrounded by green mountains with names I will never learn. The house is pretty, big enough for everyone to visit, the dogs reassure me with their reliable doggy ways. Days begin and end, weeks come and go, only my focus is small and intense: Catherine. I keep forgetting all the rest—changing seasons, stories told, stories withheld, the pleasure of seeing Chuck almost every day and Catherine and her family sometimes spending their weekends here, as if I were a vacation. My daughter Jennifer visits often with Violet and Ralphie, and the four children play together, making memories. My default position remains fear.

I fear for Chuck too. He has scans of his liver every six months. He won't last forever. (I hear him saying either "Why *not?*" or "Thank God," depending on his mood.)

Today, though, I finally began worrying about someone else, an old friend gone to the dark place, someone I can't help.

"Make yourself useful," my father used to say. I forget what he wanted me to do—dust? vacuum? dishes? Nothing that appealed to me. But now I seem to be living by those words.

"You don't just *want* to be useful," Chuck points out. "You *need* to be useful."

That sounds neurotic, but I'm too old to be worrying about it. Neurosis is for the young, who think they are made of time.

So we have children finding salamanders under stones, and wanting to know the names of things, and Fred finding a locust, almost invisible on a tree, tediously making its way out of its shell. Freddy, so excited, jumping and shouting, "Isn't it *amazing*! Isn't it *amazing*!" Once the creature had worked the last of itself out, Fred carefully reached up and removed the husk. We both stared at it lying in his palm, fascinated by the hole the locust had made for its departure. We watched the newly hatched thing as it crawled up the trunk with its green legs. Then Freddy ran into the kitchen to tell his mother. "*Amazing*" I heard him cry through the open window.

Mindfulness

The dishwasher is broken. The door won't close properly. Now its lights won't turn off, it is stuck in some dysfunctional machine dream. All of my male family members who are around this weekend have a go at it, but nothing works. I don't want to fix it. Nobody (me) ever unloads the dishwasher, it is too boring and thus too onerous a job, so there are always dishes in the sink anyway, and now I am going to wash them as they appear. It is a contemplative activity. Here is the Fire King golden cup from the set my daughter Jennifer gave me. Here is the big mug my daughter Catherine uses for her tea when she drops by. Here is last night's cast-iron pan with the remnants of a roast chicken I made for Chuck. Here are the pale blue cups Kitty gave me. Here is a plate with chocolate smears from the twins' birthdays. Here are two candles with the icing sucked off.

Deer

In the back, under the fallen apple tree and hidden in the tall stalks of whatever remains of summer, lies a deer carcass. Every morning there is less and less of it. How did it get here? Maybe, as a friend suggested, the deer was hit by a car on 212 and made it as far as my yard, then lay down and died. I doubt coyotes brought it down, coyotes are mostly in the hills, the less inhabited parts of these parts, or so I hope. I never hear them. Anyway, there is this deer. My dogs can't reach it, the underground electric fence stops them, nor do they smell its remains as everything is frozen. It must take some effort to rip what is left of the flesh from what is left of its bones. Catherine loves bones, and I have rescued and hung in the fork of a tree the jawbone, teeth attached, the small ones in front very worn down. This morning there is a long piece of backbone lying by itself, and I will put that somewhere safe too until nature takes its course and all trace of pink is gone.

I keep an eye on the dogs anyway. Carolina has already wandered past the electric fence, whether she is too old and deaf to hear the warning whistle before the shock, or the weight she has lost makes the collar ineffective, it being too loose around her throat. She is an old party now, her muzzle almost completely white, her eyes getting milky. She needs help getting into bed at night.

This morning a friend called to say her husband had driven past my neighbor's yard, which borders on the very busy 212, and saw one of my dogs there. I rushed into the car, peeled out of the driveway, and stopped with a screech at the end of the road. There was Carolina, sniffing in circles, and I caught her easily, lifted her into the car, and drove the thirty yards home. Both of us were trembling.

Soup

Chuck has bought a chicken. He sounds proud. The chicken sat in his icebox for three days, wrapped in its original plastic, and now he wants to make soup. I make a worried sound.

"Better take a good sniff," I say.

"It's fine," he says. I decide not to argue.

"So throw it in a pot, chop up celery and a whole lot of carrots, cover it with cold water, and simmer it until the meat wants to fall off the bones."

"I don't have many carrots," he says.

"Go get some. The ones you cook with you can eat, but then put more in at the end to make the broth sweet." Then I tell him a terrible secret. I put a little sugar in the soup if the carrots aren't plentiful or sweet.

"You can fry up the liver for Pojd," I say. "But throw the gizzard in the soup. It is delicious with salt."

He cooks it. Then the soup sits on the back of his stove for days, but he declares it a success.

Birdsong

Catherine has a PET scan scheduled for this week. She has been in pain recently, a pain that seems to move around her body. She is scared, I am scared, we are all of us scared. I sat outside in the early morning, and heard an unfamiliar bird. It seemed to me it was saying over and over, "screaMING screaMING screaMING," but that might have been my state of mind.

After a year of bad news, there is good news. Catherine's scan is clear. There is no sign of cancer in her system. Wonderful news, a lovely day, but I don't trust good news and I don't like good weather. Dread has been my faithful companion, and without it I am alone. There has been no tearful relief, or renewed vigor. Maybe I have burned out those circuits. The sun is golden, the trees will turn green eventually, the sky is blue with a few puffy white clouds, but I don't know what to do with it, so I head inside to watch all five seasons of *Burn Notice* again. There nothing exists but these silly people running around shouting at each other, all of them carrying guns and drinking things I'd love to be drinking too. Then I watch 24. "Secure the perimeter!" "We're running out of time!"

But my behavior is troubling. Who sits in a dark room watching *Burn Notice* on a beautiful day? I've thought about it, trying to get under it, but there isn't any deep here. Just the simple desire to be not living one's life. I need to learn how to accept a clearing as a clearing. Yes, the woods are still all around us, yes, there are five years of PET scans every four months ahead of us, yes, triple negative is a monstrous disease, but this is a clearing.

There might even be a pond.

Jennifer

Jennifer calls every day after dropping the kids at school. "*Good* morning," she says in her generous, cheerful voice. This is my favorite way to start off the day. We talk on the phone as often as if we were just in the next room, little bits of our lives transferred back and forth.

Garden

Catherine is making a garden now. A friend asks her what the difference is between skunk cabbage and hostas. "Hostas look like skunk cabbage that went to private school," she says. "I'm going to write that down," I say, laughing. Catherine is recovering from radiation, planting flowers and planning a vegetable garden. For the first time, under Catherine's influence and borrowing her enthusiasm, I am planting a garden too. First I pulled out millions of nettles, whose roots snake along lengthwise underground, and threw them on a tarp. My grandson Joe hacked down and dug out a field of forsythia that was encroaching on the lawn like the topiary garden in *The Shining*. I am noticing everything: how bright a pale green are the locust leaves—almost chartreuse—before they sober up. I will go to Houst to find the color, try to make a springlike painting.

Tiny

A tiny (one-knuckle-high) tree somehow took root in the dirt between two boards of a wooden table on the patio. Catherine discovered it. In the morning it had a cap on its head, not an acorn, some other covering. Then it grew half an inch and by afternoon the cap had fallen off. Chuck came by and took its picture. We all wondered how long it would last, how high it would grow. But there wasn't enough dirt for its roots, it dwindled and died.

I tried not to think of this as an omen, but unwelcome thoughts enter my head all the time.

Loss

Chuck rarely talks about his children in terms of grief. He adores them all, is happiest, I think, when they are visiting. But every once in a while his divorce, and the damage it did, rises up and he breaks down. I remember we were out for supper one night a couple of years ago and the subject came up. I might have been talking about what my kids went through with all my divorces, and he may have been replying. It might have been one of those conversations old friends have, familiar as prayer, only this time it took a turn. I looked across the table at my weeping friend. Chuck overcome is a sight as rare as a solar eclipse.

I am aware of my cavalier attitude toward men. I wittily describe them as single-celled organisms. In the time of divorce, I take the woman's side; it's my default position. But this is too easy, and it leaves out the men I love. Chuck is one; my son, Ralph, is another.

Without any warning, Ralph's former wife decided to move with their three daughters from Vermont to Nantucket Island. Ralph was living in Montpelier, where he had been used to seeing his girls a lot, and now they may as well have been on their way to the moon. Ralph was devastated. Chuck and Catherine and I were having supper, talking about Ralph's imminent loss, and how there seemed no practical solution. Chuck began to say something about how Ralph had to find a way to hold on to them. "It's so important," Chuck began, and his voice broke. Catherine moved quickly to the sofa and put her arm around him, but there was no comfort for anyone that night.

Staples

Six staples in my ears. Acupuncture. I can't stop smoking. I want this to work so Catherine can give it a shot, but this is day three, and I've scrounged up all the butts from the studio and the rest of the house, and smoked all but three right down to the cuticle. To keep busy, I took the dogs to have baths at the vet. They have returned, silky and clean, but are now busy digging and rolling in the dust. Dust isn't so bad. It's the other stuff. Cooper's collar had a lot of deer shit on it, and I took it off and sprayed it with various things and then rubbed it and laid it in the sun, and now I need to find an old toothbrush. He's so clean I can't put it on him until it is sparkling.

They all got up at five this morning, an hour earlier than usual. I held them at bay (now I know what that means) until five-thirty, then let them out, all three howling and barking into the morning. If they weren't hounds, it might be quieter, but they are hardwired for the hunt. So far they haven't discovered the two birds' nests on my front porch, a tiny overhang that leads to the front door, which we never use. Sparrows occupy the light that hangs over the door, and robins are in the eaves.

Now it's a rainy Saturday morning, birds cheeping. God, what a lot of work it is to be a robin. Jennifer calls, having found two tiny blue jays as yet unable to fly, who are supposed to be learning how to forage and live on their own, but hers is a neighborhood full of cats and the occasional coyote. She has trapped them under flowerpots on her front porch but can't decide what to do next. She so badly wants to save them. I tell her she has to let them go.

Despite my good intentions I find a cigarette on the floor of the living room. A cigarette is to smoke, so I smoke it immediately. I feel the dark god of nicotine raise himself on one elbow in my bloodstream. *What took you so long, girl?* he asks lazily. He has those bedroom eyes.

Windows

My friend Karol has given me three superb storm windows. "Look at the tar on the edges of this one," she exclaimed. (She must be an artist too.) "I know," I said. "I love it!" My grandson Joe helped put them in the back of my car, and we drove home. They are so big I'm going to use the sawhorses for the first time. Then I'll lie underneath to see what's happening. I could get one of those rolling things people use to work under cars. I'm already imagining huge trees, their branches swooping to the ground, like the old horse chestnut in my parents' yard. The one my father called a church.

Maine

Chuck has rented a house in Maine for Ralph and his children this summer. They will be together for two weeks.

Broken

The painting I made on Karol's glass was of blue sky, white and gray and pink clouds. It wasn't a good painting, I gave it too much thought, and the glass was too large for me to control, or lose control of, whichever way you want to look at it. It lay across the sawhorses all right, but when I picked it up and held it vertically, a sound like rushing water ensued, and the glass fell to pieces at (and on) my feet. Too many heavy layers of paint, alas. When I picked up a large piece, it broke into smaller and smaller pieces. This reminded me of the conundrum of moving toward an object going only halfway each time, so that in theory you never reach it. This I never understood. Anyway, where the paint managed to hold the glass together, there was a crackled pattern, like honeycomb, and beautiful. What to do? How to use this? I chose a few pieces and glued them to a sheet of blue glass, so that the lighter sky and clouds float on the surface, and despite the strict instructions on the glue none of which told you how to glue painted glass to glass, the pieces are holding.

A Life

Catherine says now she has to figure out what to do with her life. For more than a year she has been focused on chemotherapy, surgeries, radiation. Cancer. A tightrope burning under her feet. Suddenly she is in the clear. "I don't know what to do," she said the other day.

"Whatever you want," I probably said.

But what is harder than that? What do we do when there's a before and you don't know what to do with the after? And that awful phrase bangs around in the back of my mind: "likely to recur."

It occurs to me that I have the same problem.

So What to Do

I'm watching DVDs of a program called *Supernatural*. I learned about it at Catherine's one cold gray morning when I stopped for a visit. She was lying on the couch with her two ancient cats watching this terrible thing about demons and werewolves and shape-shifters, a whole world infested with vicious beings after the Hellmouth was opened by accident. "How can you watch this?" I asked, settling down next to her, gluing myself to the screen. "It's terrible. It's everything you hate in a movie." Catherine long ago announced her aversion to movies that were "dark and wet." This is dark and wet. Very dark, very wet. Everything is dripping with ectoplasm or sodden with blood.

"It's good," she says, not taking her eyes off the television.

It is ten in the morning. Granted, outside it is nasty, depressing, cold. But television at this hour? I am shocked. I stay for three episodes. "I've got to get out of here," I say, standing up resolutely. "I can't get hooked on this stuff, and it's very upsetting." She nods and smiles, continuing to watch.

"Oh, stay for one more episode," she says.

I went home and two days later bought all seven seasons of this show and the eighth is on order. Like drinking, I start watching earlier and earlier each day. I'm learning all sorts of useful things for when the Apocalypse arrives. I learn you have to put salt on your windowsills and doorways to keep the demons out. I learn what instrument kills what evil being. Some need their heads chopped off with an iron ax, some need to be burned alive, some need silver bullets or wooden stakes. Two very good-looking brothers have teamed up to fight the powers of evil, but they have issues with each other. At first Catherine's favorite was Dean, the older brother, and I liked Sam. Now it's the other way around. I have memorized the license plate of their old Chevy Impala, and plan to use it as a password.

It's easy to find that five or six hours have sped by without my noticing. I am having fun. This is not my world, these are not my fears. *Supernatural* is great storytelling, and it is not my story.

Out of the Blue

Catherine tells me that long ago, she was lying on the Amagansett beach when suddenly, out of nowhere, a dark cloud swept across, there and gone in less than a minute. "Everything changed," she tells me. "The color of the sea, the taste of the air, the air itself, the feel of the sand, the temperature, everything, and then it was gone and the day was hot and blue again, the ocean turned back into the right color."

This is the kind of memory I have always thought needs to be remembered by someone else, after the original owner is gone. I'll never forget it.

Bad Daphne

Daphne, who weighs maybe sixty pounds, thinks she is a lapdog. She climbs up wherever I am and, like mercury, melts into whatever space there is. Or isn't. Her warmth is comforting, her head on my shoulder, or deep in the back of the chair behind me, and she falls asleep. But when it comes time for me to get up, she doesn't understand that when the human being begins to squirm, that's the cue for the dog to get up too. It requires more strength than I have to heave myself up while she lies sprawled on me, oblivious, but somehow the job gets done and she slides in surprise to the floor.

Daphne is the kind of dog you could do anything to, you could jump on her, you could pull on her lovely ears, anything, and she wouldn't object. But this morning she discovered one of the deer's leg bones, stripped of flesh, hoof attached. Some animal must have dragged it out onto the lawn last night. When I approach her to take it away, she growls and snarls.

I am proud of her.

The only time I have been even mildly irritated with Daphne was this morning when I woke to discover big holes in my new blue sheet, and a bigger hole in the mattress pad, its cottony innards distributed all over the floor. I have had this mattress pad for a long time. I don't feel sentimental, but it does have its visible history. It endured Harry's inadvertent peeing, something else's vomit, other leakages I can't easily explain, all manner of grunge from dogs that got ground into it despite 350-thread-count sheets, and an explosion of blue from a ballpoint pen, which is fading to purple, like a bruise, after many washings. This was due to my grandson Joe's drawing-in-bed habits, when he lived here some years ago. Also many small black specks I examined compulsively hoping to find them inanimate, which they were.

Mattress pads are expensive, the choices bewildering. Which to choose? Why do they cost so much? Looking through catalogs, I find that most of the comfiest ones appear to be composed of something Daphne would love to sink her teeth into. And a feather bed is out of the question, alluring though it may look; it's too much money, and I can already envision its contents floating in air and dusting the floor.

"*Bad* Daphne," I said. She rolled on her back, feet up, ready to play.

Googling

I don't remember what this particular assignment was, but a woman in one of my memoir classes wrote about an old love, the one that got away, the one she had thought about, daydreamed about, wondered about for years. She found him on Facebook, and wrote him. They planned to meet at a restaurant in New York. She laid out all her clothes on the bed and tried everything on before she settled on what to wear. She bought new shoes. She had her hair cut. She probably put on blush. Then she took the bus to Manhattan. She is seventy.

Her old love was every bit as nice as she recalled. They had a pleasant time, they talked about what had and what hadn't happened, they talked about what their lives had been like. They drank wine. He told her he had been devastated when she left him to marry another man. But he was heavy and bald and had been happily married for years.

How on earth can anyone survive without a daydream? I wondered.

"What a terrible loss," I said. "How can you stand it?"

"We can be friends now," she said.

Before I got pregnant and married and my life zigged off in an unexpected direction, there was another boy I loved. He was handsome and kind and sexy and gentle. We met on the Amagansett beach, where I'd gone every summer of my life. Everyone knew everyone else, but this boy was a stranger. He looked almost like a man. I was seventeen, and looking good, and I got up and strolled into the water as nonchalantly as possible what with my heart beating so fast. I dove through a wave, and when I surfaced there he was. His eyes were merry, but they were old, as if he knew things I'd never know, but life still amused him.

I googled this old love, to reassure myself that he was still there somewhere, and perhaps remembered us those years ago. Although we hadn't seen each other in over fifty years, and we had never slept together, I felt close to him. Sure enough, there he was on his own website, complete with email address. I wrote him a short note, ending with "I used to daydream about you a lot, a long time ago." He wrote back. He said he remembered the first time he saw me. "You walked down the beach and into the ocean," he said. This made me smile. "It was an electrifying moment. I followed you. We rode some waves. We made a date for that night. My next memory is of you leaning against a tree and pulling my body into yours in an embrace and kiss that I've never forgotten." He said some more things, all of them nice. He too is happily married, has kids and probably grandkids.

He remembered what I remembered. It was like being on that beach again, seventeen years old. I could taste the air, see the blue of the water, remember the heat. I printed out his email. I lay around for hours daydreaming, a welcome remove from reality.

Then the lovely youthful feeling floated out of reach. I was seventy-one again, not seventeen. But I folded my friend's email and put it in the special section of my wallet where I keep my Medicare card. It goes with me everywhere. Sometimes, on rainy days when I feel unlovely, I read it.

Speaking of Amagansett

My grandmother's house is for sale for $3.3 million. It hasn't been ours for years. She bought it in the nineteen forties for $11,000. It used to be an inn, but that was before my grandmother's time. There are eight bedrooms on the second floor. Nobody has made an offer. The only heat comes from an enormous grate on the floor of the dining room. My sisters and I used to love to stand there on cold mornings, our nightgowns billowing up.

I think of it as my grandmother's, because it's that kind of house, the kind you claim, or perhaps claims you. It's the second on the left, the one with the wide gray porch. I still have dreams where I'm sweeping leaves off that porch, leaves from the elms that disappeared in the fifties, whether felled by a hurricane or done in by disease I can't remember. It doesn't matter—those are the leaves I will sweep until I die and the memory dies with me. At the end of the road is the Atlantic Ocean. My family moved often, but every summer we went back to that house where nothing changed. The sheets always smelled of lavender, the parlor was always as hushed as church, the library, a small crooked room whose walls were lined with books, was the place the grown-ups gathered every afternoon for drinks. Pink gins.

The smell of privet, all those giant bushes that lined the road to the beach, is the smell of summer. Yes, there were roses, the split-rail fence we walked on barefoot was covered with wild climbing roses, but the smell that overwhelmed me was the blossoming privet.

The kindhearted real estate agent let me walk through, because if it doesn't sell soon, the present owner will tear it down. Nothing personal: it's a question of money. The land may be more valuable without the house. It doesn't matter how old the structure is (196 years), or how wide the floorboards, or how delicate the tracery on all the hinges of all the doors. It no longer matters which room my grandmother died in, or that she kept red geraniums on the kitchen windowsills. Nothing matters anymore except the money. Not the transoms, not the peeling wallpaper in the tiny rooms in three corners of the attic, not the beautiful banister, not the cold back bedroom that said, as soon as you were settled, *Get up get up get up*, and you did. The darkness of the steep back stairs, what happens to that? It doesn't matter. If the house doesn't sell by next month, the whole thing comes down. I walked through every room, the bones of the house were the same as I remembered. All the doorways in the right places, the windows.

My daughter Sarah came with me, bringing her camera. It was afternoon, there was a familiar square of light on the parlor floor, a few scraps of furniture here and there. Sarah took a picture in one of the empty rooms. I am headed toward the door, my face turned to the camera. I am expressionless, my body a blur. There is a strange fog by the window.

The house has been torn down. Nothing is left but the old white fence. There used to be privet bushes everywhere. "The smell of privet is the smell of summer for me," I say to Catherine.

"Yes, Mom," she says, "I know. Your memories are my memories now."

Sarah

Sarah snuck back in the middle of the night and removed the long wooden banister, polished by a hundred and fifty years of hands, carrying it away like a family heirloom. Sarah can do anything she sets her mind to, even if it means breaking the laws of physics.

Irony

I read *On the Road* for the first time when I was sixty-eight. I should have read it when I was young, because what struck me was how heartbreakingly innocent it was, and how boring. I was puzzled until it hit me that there wasn't any irony in there. Was innocence the opposite of irony? I became obsessed. What is irony? Where did it come from? When did it take over? How do we get rid of it? I asked Chuck if he thought irony was an enhancement of life or a scrim that keeps us at a remove. He said maybe irony is the lens through which we see the picture in reverse. I wrote that down. Sometimes I think one thing, sometimes another. These days I'm apt to think of irony as a suit of armor.

"Wit distances us," said Northrop Frye. I have Chuck's copy of *Anatomy of Criticism*. He gave it to me years ago, when I was feeling ignorant, assuring me it was easier than I thought, and interesting. I love his notes in the margins. I will never give it back. If he asks, I will say I lost it.

I plan a day where I wake up and eschew all ironic casts of thought. I will do everything directly, look everything in the eye, take it at face value, experience one thing at a time. A Day Without Irony, I imagine a new national holiday. This morning I settle on the porch, looking out at the yard, the mountain beyond, absorbing yellow leaves and blue sky and green grass; the moment extends itself. The radio is on in the next room providing white noise. I have the dogs with me, and I am doing very well until eight words distinguish themselves from all others on the radio: "one hundred strands of hair from Che Guevara . . ."

It turns out that his hair is being auctioned off. His *hair*. Not only was the man executed, but years later his hair is being sold by capitalist pigs. I assume they are capitalists although perhaps not pigs. Perhaps they are putting their children through school.

I have various unformed thoughts about irony, thoughts that have not reached what I think of as the soft ball stage (using a metaphor from cooking fudge). To continue the cooking metaphor, I have had the epiphany which may be nothing more than having reinvented the wheel, that equal parts of innocence shaken up with equal parts of experience, like salad dressing, make, no matter how hard you resist it, irony, if the bubbles of innocence separate after a while from those of experience. If they mix completely you probably wind up with cynicism. But wait, what about wisdom? Wisdom, I decide, looking again at those yellow leaves, lies in the decision to mix up a fresh batch every morning.

A Dream

All my dogs were lost and then one by one they came back, my Rosie among them. She was healthy and beautiful. How surprised and delighted I was to see her! I had completely forgotten she died. We lay down together to sleep, and I stroked her lovely body, and she laid her head on my shoulder as she often did. When one of the other dogs came near, she snarled. My Rosie. When I woke, she was gone. I have collected river stones to put on her grave. "Thank you," I say over and over, placing them on the slab of bluestone that is her grave.

Losing It

This morning after waking up at five with the dogs, I went back to bed at nine for a little pick-me-up nap. I lay under the red comforter, Daphne lying next to me, her head on my stomach. I felt peaceful. Thoughts and stories went in and out of my head. My memory, I decided, is not a meadow, not the view from a hill, or even a city street. My memory is an archipelago. I then pictured an archipelago, thousands of small islands forming something whose shape I could not determine, resting as I was under the comforter, too happy to think straight. (Happiness seems not to require a full set of marbles.) Other thoughts came in and out, disintegrating like smoke before I could get hold of them, and I began to think that losing track of oneself, entering the stage where you couldn't remember much of anything that made sense, might be pleasant, as long as the loss was at a distance, a speck on the horizon to arouse curiosity, not dismay. I will explain this to my family, before I forget.

Exercise in Futility

A very small woodpecker is beating his brains out against a piece of metal on the telephone pole across the street. Bangbangbangbangbang. I stand underneath. "There are no bugs in there," I call up to him, "you're going to blunt your beak," but he keeps hammering away. We have a lot of woodpeckers. Great big ones, and the noise they make is very loud. Maybe this poor baby thinks he's doing it right. There's a lesson in this somewhere, and I hope I've already learned it.

"I can't even guess what the lesson is," says Chuck, having taken this in.

"He thinks he sounds cool. He doesn't care if he isn't getting anywhere."

"Maybe he's just persistent. Maybe he's a percussionist."

You are so obstinate, I think.

"Maybe he thinks it should yield to his awesome power."

"I think you just finished it for me," I say.

"I don't think so," says Chuck.

The end.

Whereabouts

After a nap or in the middle of the night I wake up and realize I have no idea what town I'm in or what street I live on. Which direction are my feet pointing, which way is north, where are the windows and doors in this bedroom? It takes me a moment, but then there are the warm bodies and sweet snores of my dogs, and I know it doesn't really matter where I am.

Bad Dog

Sadie used to live next door. The man who took care of her couldn't keep her in the yard. She craved freedom, I guess. He put in a stockade fence. She got out. He buried cement blocks under the fence. She got out. He put chicken wire on top of the fence. She got out. He sat on the roof for three hours, watching to see how she did it. She stayed in.

She came trotting over here if I was home. She jumped into my lap if I was sitting outside. She pushed through the dog door if I was inside. She once arrived breathless with two inches of chewed-off leash still attached to her collar. How not to love a dog like this? She barked loudly one dark rainy night, and I found her on the kitchen steps, soaked and shivering. I let her in, dried her off, and she slept with us. It was a lovely night.

But she had once been found miles away on the Wittenberg Road barking at somebody's chickens. She had been seen wandering down Route 212, which is a busy road. I worried about her. Every time her owner picked her up, I worried about the next time she'd escape. What if I was away? I began wondering how I could secretly just keep her. But I couldn't come up with a decent plan.

Her owner loved her too, and was determined to outfox her. "I'll take her," I began suggesting, when I sensed his growing frustration. "I have the underground fence, and she'll be safe." He shook his head, taking the reluctant little thing home. "What if she gets hit by a car?" I said, desperate. "Well," said this otherwise

perfectly nice man, "if she gets hit, she gets hit. That's her fate."
I grumbled to all my kids. How could anyone say such a thing?
But he had been struggling for years to keep her safe. He was
getting calls from neighbors, from police, from the ASPCA. It
was so clear to me that I should adopt her, why couldn't he see
this? I offered $300 for the scamp. But he was not going to be
bested by a little black dog that weighed maybe eighteen pounds.
He nicknamed her Houdini and took her home, time after time.

Then one day he called. I could have her. School was starting,
he teaches at night, and he couldn't possibly keep running to pick
her up wherever she was that wasn't here with me. He said I was
probably better for her than the pound, where he had once, in
exasperation, threatened to take her. She was mine? Sadie was
mine? I had a moment of elation and terror. What had I gotten
myself into?

Sadie has been here almost a year. According to her vet
records, she is half Lab and half boxer. I see no sign of either. She
has chewed up two sofas, four chairs, innumerable socks, and
several books. She has destroyed four ottomans. Anything left
on the floor is hers, including rugs, and I warn visitors not to take
off their shoes. She has eaten three comforters, once Daphne's
specialty. She nips the back legs of whichever dog is in front of
her on the way downstairs. She relentlessly teases Daphne, who
went from pup to matron almost overnight. When another dog
seeks attention, she sidles him or her out of the way. If Daphne
gets on my lap (and Daphne is a big girl), Sadie jumps up too,
and they find a way to share me as I struggle to breathe. As I read
this over I don't know how I stand it. If I didn't love this dog so
much, she'd be dead.

My friend Nona suggested I get her a ThunderShirt. This is a comfy soft jacket that fits the way swaddling clothes fit, and is meant to make an anxious dog feel safe. It worked for two days. Then I taught an afternoon class, was gone for hours, and came home to find a cushion off the little rose-colored chair in hundreds of pieces. I'm not sure Sadie is an anxious dog, exactly. She just doesn't like it when I leave. Maybe, as several people have suggested, she needs Prozac. Maybe she needs a crate, or training, or spring to arrive. Meanwhile, I use a spray bottle of water to stop her when she won't quit bothering Daphne. It works pretty well.

After a tiring day of destruction, she sits on my lap and puts her forepaws on my chest. Then she stares intently at my face. She licks my nose. Sometimes she snorts directly *into* my nose and I get a brief and mysterious high. When we go to bed, she fits herself in the crook of my arm, lays her head on my shoulder.

And she sleeps.

Blue Skies

After Catherine's diagnosis, when I began to paint again, I went back to painting woods, dark woods you wouldn't want to enter alone. She has had clear scans twice now. Now all I paint are skies. Blue skies, white clouds. Every scrap of glass becomes a sky. There is a bit of blue sky on my left foot. My hands are blue.

I mention this to Catherine.

"If there is a connection here," says Catherine, smiling, "I don't think you have to look very far to find it."

A New Perspective

When Catherine got cancer, I stopped teaching. After her year of treatment I started again. This workshop is for people who have had cancer, and those who are living with cancer. We started small and were supposed to run for five weeks, but our numbers have grown, and the workshop has been going strong now for almost two years.

I run this class differently. We don't discuss in depth the work of two people a week; we don't have that kind of time. Roughly half the group have metastatic cancer, and we want to hear from everyone every week, so this class relies on doing exercises. Everyone reads, every week.

This may be a workshop, but I'm the one learning. Part of what I've learned is that if it isn't life and death, it isn't life and death. I have learned that every moment is precious. I know now that cancer is not an isolated experience; cancer is part of life. I have learned that to be witness to one another's lives is the greatest of gifts. Thursday afternoons are sacred. Carol Dwyer, one of the writers, puts it perfectly: "Our bonds are quickened by the proximity of death," she says.

Catherine is part of a larger landscape now, and it comforts me.

More About Naps

I like a cold room at bedtime. If it's winter. I turn the heat off, open the window, and turn on the fan. My hands are ice-cold when I read, my feet, which I like to stick out of the covers, also ice-cold. I love this. The dogs are comfortably under the covers, so most of the rest of me is warm. I pull in my extremities after I turn off the light.

In the morning my floor is cold, the room is windy, I can't find shoes or socks, and I have no slippers (Daphne). The urge to lunge back into the warm bed is mighty. But the dogs need to go out. Some days, these short winter days, I am up only a fraction of the day, all the rest of it is spent napping. "Napping" is not the right word for sleep that is interrupted occasionally by an hour of being awake, then back to bed.

Surely there is more to life than all this sleeping. I believe in naps. I believe they clear the mind. But my first nap begins an hour after getting up in the morning. If the dogs wake at five, then going back to bed is not unreasonable. But if you get up at eight, then going back to bed at nine can only be depressing. I am beginning, I think, to turn into a solid.

Here are some of the rules I have made for myself.

Get dressed immediately, that's key. If you make coffee and let the dogs out and wait for them to come back in while still in your pajamas, you are still technically in bed. Do not wait too long to turn the heat back on, or you will go back to bed just to "get warm." When you go upstairs to get dressed, do *not* get into bed "for a minute" even though the dogs are looking at you hope-fully. Remember, you are not a dog. Do not even *sit* on the bed except to pull your pants on (because standing on one leg has become precarious). If you should fall back under the covers, try not to be too upset when the next time you open your eyes it is noon. Get dressed and put on a bra and something too tight that will be uncomfortable to lie down in. Be cheered when you pick up the phone to call your kids and realize it is only 11:55. Listen to your daughter who will remind you that at seventy-one you have earned this. "Give yourself a break," she will say, and you say you will try. Then hang up and pick up the business section of the newspaper you put on the rug yesterday to sop up the pee. Then remove the sports section you put under the rug so the pee would not discolor the floor. Look around for the bottle of stuff that eliminates odors even though nothing smells yet. Re-member that summer brings out every secret. Pick up the towel Daphne has been shredding. Put the dishes away.

Get out of the house.

Napping is divine, but I no longer have all the time in the world.

March

Here we are at the beginning of spring again, the weather is not cold, but I am. Chuck drops by while I am sitting outside writing in the sun, shivering. "Spring is horrible," I tell him. "I'm freezing all the time."

Chuck is too. He turns his heat way up. "Money means nothing to me," he is fond of saying.

"I saw my neighbor in her garden today." I point to a house just visible through trees. "She was bending down. I think she was gardening."

"That's what gardening consists of," says Chuck. "A lot of bending down."

He suggests I write about the positions we are no longer capable of assuming. "Kneeling," he says. "And putting on socks," he continues, "the chair can't be too high."

"Oh, I have one of those," I say. "It was my mother's. It's the little one with roses on it. Women had them in their bedrooms for getting dressed. Slipper chairs."

Then I remember an insight I had when I woke up this morning. The words "yo" and "like" (when beginning a sentence) are not parts of speech at all! They are *punctuation*. "It's like starting a sentence with a comma," I tell Chuck, "isn't that brilliant?"

"With a little refinement," he answers, "it might achieve the level of a thought."

We decide to drive to the SPCA in Kingston. Our friend Susan has told Chuck about a basset hound they've got. Chuck is willing to go look even though his dog, Pojd, is a handful. "Another dog might make her friskier," I say. We gaze at her lying flat on the flagstones, asleep in the sun. "I'm not sure I want her friskier," says Chuck.

The SPCA is closed, but some of the dogs are out in their tiny yards, and one of them is the enormous basset, trumpeting away. Chuck stands in front of him, saying something I can't hear. I wander down a couple of cages where three small puppies are leaping and barking. I want them. Every one of them! There is a brown one, a white and brown one, and a darker brindle one! Their little ears flop over like wontons! Their curling tails wag crazily! They are leaping and yipping with joy and hope! I want all of them right now this minute! A moment passes. The reality of six dogs sinks in.

Good thing it's Monday, we agree. Otherwise there might be a basset in the back and three puppies in the front.

As we round a bend on the Sawkill, something is flying across the road, although flight implies speed and grace, and this creature's motion is more accurately described as lumbering through the air. The road is too curvy to turn around and we are left with the memory of a round yellowish feathery ball flapping small blunt wings and a tail that resembles the spine of a fish, or a snake. A ridiculous, if slightly menacing creature about a foot long. Part bird, part insect, part fish, part reptile.

When we told Catherine, she began googling "strange creatures Ulster County." She looked up everything she could think of: "birds with tails like snake skeletons," "birds with blunt wings," "odd birds of the Northeast." Nothing turned up. I began to think what we saw was a mythological being, out of his element or out of his time, put together by an angry god or a Senate subcommittee, never to be seen again.

Dumplings in March

We were supposed to get a lot of snow last night. Warnings were up everywhere, instructions on how to survive. Water, flashlights, et cetera, et cetera.

I bought a Campanelli's chicken from Woodstock Meats and a lot of carrots and celery. I made chicken soup with dumplings but found I had only a tiny bit of flour when the recipe called for two cups. So I improvised. The "dumplings" dissolved into the broth. Chuck came over and we watched three episodes of something. Or rather, I did. Chuck fell asleep on the couch, after making room for Carolina at his feet. As usual. When I finally woke him at midnight, he rose stiffly, asking what he'd missed. "Nothing," I say. "Everything."

We have a deal. When he starts driving home from a day of work in the city he calls me as he leaves, and I call him every hour after that to make sure he's alert. It worries me how tired he is.

The soup was rich and delicious, but I'll never be able to make it again.

Trust Binds Us

The other day, apropos of what I can't remember, Chuck said, "We are bound by trust." He was speaking philosophically.

But yes, I thought. We are.

Drinking and Thinking

There are three things that make me want to drink: difficult times, when I want alcohol to either alleviate the pain or allow me to feel it; clear days that make me want to scribble all over the irritating blue sky; and well, waking up in the morning. I'm an alcoholic. I've quit before, but always started up again, usually in the kitchen. I'd find myself pouring half a bottle of red wine into tomato sauce, then testing for flavor, using a ladle and scooping up only the wine part, then pouring the rest of the bottle in and testing again. This gave me the tiniest buzz, and of course it wasn't really *drinking*.

But brownies were my downfall. You have to put vanilla in brownies or there's no point, and I've always scoffed at recipes that call for a measly teaspoon. A teaspoon? I'd pour half a bottle into the mixture, then taste. Soon I was drinking it straight out of the bottle. Vanilla is delicious, and it's also 35 percent alcohol.

Good old lowly old vanilla.

I became a vanilla connoisseur. It started with McCormick, which is too sweet, moved on to Durkee, which has a bitter finish, attempted Goya, which was surprisingly bland, then discovered Madagascar Bourbon vanilla. Now here was a really *robust* vanilla, and it was organic! I began going to different grocery stores, imagining the clerks whispering to each other, "Didn't she just buy four bottles of vanilla yesterday?" I alternated between the West Side Market, the University Market, and whatever is now a Gristedes. I discovered the Eighty-Sixth Street Williams-Sonoma and traveled crosstown to buy a dozen bottles at a time, twelve-ouncers, murmuring something about getting my Christmas shopping done early, then slinking out the door, hailing a taxi, sliding down in the seat, unscrewing the cap off a bottle, and glugging it all the way home. *Vanilla isn't drinking,* I told myself; *if you can't order it at a bar, it isn't drinking.* The fact that you can get hammered on a big bottle of vanilla meant nothing.

I love to drink. I love the taste. Wherever I've lived, I've found the place that makes the best Manhattans. Up here, it's Cucina. I love the dappled place I find myself after one drink, and even two, but after three I'm getting lost in the woods, after four, I'm climbing back onto the barstool I've just fallen off of. After that, I stagger to the car to be driven home by Chuck. The point is that after one drink, there's no stopping.

Six months after Ralph talked sense to me, I decided one beer a day would be okay, as long as I could keep it to one beer a day. I went to the Cub every afternoon, bought my one bottle of Rochefort 10 and a pack of Camels. All was going smoothly until the week I was invited out for dinner four nights in a row. Out for dinner was always a different story, like being on a plane, where calories don't count. (Not that there's anything to eat on a plane anymore, but you know what I mean.) So there I was at Cucina ordering a Manhattan, then another, and often another, then three glasses of wine with dinner, and for dessert an Irish coffee (Irish on the side, please, wink wink) and I was plastered. Four nights in a row.

On the fifth morning I woke not so much with a hangover, as with appalling feelings of guilt and shame and fear. For no reason! I didn't attack anyone, I didn't take my clothes off or hurl abuse, I behaved very nicely except for a little spilling, and possibly leaning too close to Chuck, but he knows me drunk and finds a way to tolerate it. I was beside myself. *"I'm seventy-one,"* I stormed around the house shouting, *"why can't I drink?"* So I sent an urgent email to my friend Kitty asking her please to call me. And within five minutes she was on the phone. I love Kitty.

"I am so angry," I said. "I'm seventy-one years old, why can't I have a few drinks? Why do I feel so guilty and afraid and full of dread in the morning? I behaved myself! Why do I feel this horrible guilt?"

I was furious, but it was Kitty I called, Kitty, who has been sober for eleven years and counting. Kitty, who has a sense of humor, whose advice might go my way. "Go ahead," she might have said, or so I thought, but she didn't. "I feel so guilty in the morning," I whined.

"Well," she said slowly, "maybe you ought to take a look at that."

And so, at long last, I did. The other times I'd quit had been different. I remember standing on the island at 112th Street and Broadway thirty years ago, a bag of groceries in my arms, waiting for the light to change. It was the day after a Twelfth Night office party where I had hit my head against a hanging plant and pinned someone to the wall explaining rather aggressively how to cook rice, then later leaned against the front door making out with the host while his wife and everyone else looked on. *Gee, I'd* thought, *I don't really want to do that again,* and quit before the light turned green. But now, at seventy-one, I finally had to *think* about it. I do not want to feel this way, especially from something I'm doing to myself. So I have stopped, thoughtfully this time, weighing the morning against the dubious pleasure of the night before, and so far the morning is winning.

Landfill

The backyard now belongs to dogs. Huge holes dug everywhere, bits of yogurt cups obtained from counters and chewed into little bits, god knows what else. "Park-like grounds," offered the sales sheet when I bought the house. Not anymore. Now it's landfill. But the newly replanted forsythia is drooping. You know you're in trouble when even that unkillable, unstoppable bush looks languid, so I go out every morning and water. I don't want anything to die.

Here is some of what I've found in the yard. Not my cell phone, alas, Daphne has probably chewed what she wanted and left it somewhere, but I've searched both yard and house with no luck. What I did find was a small porcelain shoe that belonged to my grandmother. It was on one of the shelves of my bookcase along with other odds and ends that struck my fancy—old photographs, bits of scrap iron, pebbles, and a shell—and I guess Daphne found it irresistible, although it wasn't chewed, just deposited on the lawn near my weather vane. I don't know how I wound up with it, but the belongings of the dead are parceled out one way or another until finally you're just tossing things into boxes willy-nilly. I pick it up and look at it carefully and notice for the first time that it was mended once—glue holds the high heel on. My grandmother must have loved this little object of gilt and roses. It lives on the mantel now, far from Daphne's reach. I want to keep safe something my grandmother loved.

I have one pair of shoes left, my good shoes. Daphne has taken the others, distributed them around the yard in disrepair, even my Crocs, which she can't bite through, are gone. Well, one of them is gone. Now when I traipse through the wet to my studio, it is in my good shoes. When I take them off, I put them on the mantel with my TV remotes (both of which have bite marks), and my cigarette lighter, and whatever I'm reading. Daphne can't reach the mantel. At least not yet. Last week a friend loaned me her special copy of *Wolf Hall*. It is a first edition, first English printing. I tried not to take it, but she pressed me. It seemed churlish to refuse. So I borrowed it, read about twenty pages, and foolishly left it on the coffee table while I made a cup of coffee. The next thing I knew, Daphne had chewed at the binding of this precious (I didn't yet know how precious) book. I couldn't give it back in this condition and set about trying to find another. The only place I found a first edition first printing was on Amazon UK, and it cost $467. I bought it, and hope it will arrive soon, and I've got my eye out for its delivery. Sometimes UPS leaves things on the side porch, where they are usually found by Daphne, who is turning out to be the most expensive dog I've ever had.

Lesion

A new MRI for Chuck. He avoids my questions. Catherine tells me she had to ask four different ways before she got an answer. There appears to be a lesion on his liver. "It's not a bad thing or a good thing," he said, "but they want to schedule another MRI in three months instead of six."

"I hate the word 'lesion,'" I say to her.

"So do I," she answers.

That night Chuck and I go out for supper at Cucina. We go so often that they automatically give us a dessert if we haven't ordered one, and it's always butterscotch budino, which is our favorite. "It's on the house," the waitress says, and we dig in.

Chuck is more serious than usual. "I should be experiencing things," he says. "I should travel." I know he is thinking of the lesion. "Want to go somewhere?"

"Sure," I say. "How about Istanbul?" He mentioned Turkey one day last week. "The Greek islands? Oslo?" I have been reading a Danish detective novel. "They have fjords there."

Chuck points out that Oslo is in Norway. I'm reminded that Catherine once said to a Dutch guy, "Do you speak Hollish?"

"Anyway, not abroad. Somewhere here," he says. We eat the dessert. I order my espresso.

"How about the Grand Canyon?" I ask, but he shakes his head. "Too crowded." He wants to drive up the coast of California.

"Big Sur," I say now, and he looks up, interested. I natter on about its beauty, although I've never even seen a picture of Big

Sur. I rarely see Chuck as vulnerable as he seems tonight. When I get home, I look up Big Sur. I find places to stay. But by morning the mood has vanished, and Chuck doesn't want to go anywhere.

I suppose it's just as well. Sometimes when we travel together I am awkward. It feels as if we are short the next thing, but sex is the only next thing I know and it isn't sex. When we are home we see each other almost every day. There is no need for anything more than how comfortable we are in each other's company; we can drop in on each other any time of day or night and be welcome. But traveling, I have sometimes wanted to grab his hand, or put my arm around him. I can't get past the impulse and don't know what to do with it. So I hug him.

Transplant List

Now when Chuck talks about his own health, he speaks carefully. He doesn't want to alarm me or perhaps himself, and his voice is measured as he explains his condition. His doctor is thinking about putting him on the transplant list. This is terrifying, no matter how the news is delivered. I say something calm in return.

"I'll take care of you," I say. "When you come home."

"I know," he says.

Too Much

Yesterday, May first, there was too much green and pink and yellow. There was no escaping the loveliness, the delicacy. Beauty assaulted me on every front—forsythia, like a breaking wave, no, a tsunami of yellow; the old magnolia exploding into pink and white, like grenades; blue sky—there was no escape from all this beauty, I was being force-fed a spring morning, even the oxygen was divine, so finally I went inside and watched *The Exorcist*.

What Survives

I ask Chuck what he thinks happens when we die.
   "You live on only insofar as others continue to think about you. Then you fade and blink out."
   Fade and blink out. I think I can live with that.

Dog Envy

It is raining hard today. The dogs come in one by one, soaking wet. I dry them each with a towel, and they stand patiently until I stop. Then they give themselves violent shakes and water sprays all over and I find myself wishing I could do that, it might solve all my problems, this shaking shimmy for which there is no human equivalent.

Big Mom's Macaroni

Today I made my grandmother's macaroni. It is put together with four cheeses: Manchego, Gouda, Cheddar, and Jarlsberg. I heat up a cup of heavy cream, a cup of half-and-half, and a bunch of grated Parmesan. Big Mom knew what was good. I layer the macaroni and the cheeses, then pour the creamy liquid all over and bake it at 325 degrees so nothing curdles.

We eat and eat. Catherine has brought salad greens from her farm share, Chuck makes salad dressing. Catherine adds too much salt to the dressing, so I slice a new potato and drop it in. They are both amazed at this bit of kitchen lore, to discover that potato absorbs extra salt. I can feel my stock go up. We watch *Supernatural* (of course) until Catherine has to go home to the boys. She and Chuck split the leftovers.

"Never make this again, Mom," she says the next day. "I ate it all."

And

I got up at six because of the dogs and turned on the radio, which is my habit even before coffee and cigarette, and listened to the BBC talk with experts about fungi, which are the largest living things on the planet, and how they war with each other when competing for space and their fight sends special things into the air that can be measured, and I thought, *Well, there's the next horror novel,* and then I remembered a dream I had last night about two elks dead in my backyard and how I feared the dogs would find them and turn feral and how long it would take such huge animals to disappear and how desperate my dogs would be to get at them and they lay dead in the same spot under the apple trees where a deer had died last winter, a creature I had come to think of as my deer, and how that animal was dismantled and eaten over the course of a week until not a scrap was left unused, which reminded me that I want to be sent to a body farm when I die and then I remembered the elks woke up, and *Oh god,* I thought, *two great big elks, not threatening necessarily but certainly inconvenient,* and as I locked my doors a big man I mistook for a farmer appeared saying he knew how to deal with the two big elks and I thought that meant a nice elk farm somewhere but it turned out later he chopped their heads off, presenting me with completely smooth bloodless stumps reminding me of chopped-down trees and I was stunned and sorry and then my red plastic timer went off although I hadn't touched it, which didn't alarm me as strange things happen in this house, and then I remembered sex again, because a student had said she first made love with her husband in a cottage across from a cemetery where there was a huge statue of an elk and now whenever she thought of sex she thought of the elk or maybe it was the other way around. So there were several things to mull over: that the fungi are what we most want to watch out for even though they are doomed to extinction before we find and label them all, and that death for me is a turning into something useful because not a scrap of the deer is left, and that perhaps "my deer" meant "my dear," and that elks replaced my dear.

I opened the door where the sun was at last shining and found it was still cold, so I took a shower and put on an old black dress instead of thinking about the teaching aspect of a writing life, which I had meant to mull over this morning, expecting I would have looked up the root of "teach" by now but haven't. I look at my bookcase, and there is the fossilized bag of marshmallows my grandson wanted to put on his mother's birthday cake and I said yes.

Earlier I lay in bed thinking about how I'd been raised on superstition and despite having spent most of my life touching wood all had gone terribly wrong anyway and I now spurn and despise those rituals and then I wondered whether if I had been raised in a church or a synagogue or a mosque or a Buddhist monastery I would now be angry at a useless god, but never got out of bed to write it down and figure that out, but this morning I did start writing about the elk.

Why?

Death, it seems, death, which is always in the back of my mind because Rich was hit by a car and my daughter had cancer and my closest friend has a dying liver and other people I love have faced death and are again facing it although now death is in the room with them and how I used to be afraid of death just because it was death but now I am afraid to die in case my darlings need me.

Outside the dogs are howling.

And this is my most selfish thought, that if I lose the people I love what is left of my own life will consist only of grief.

Inconclusion

I'm sitting on the sofa with Carolina, who is snoring gently next to me, my elbow on her soft haunch as I doodle, waiting for something profound to enter my mind. Outside the birds are squawking, the little woodpecker is still working on the metal plate, the butterfly bush is moving in the breeze, and somewhere underground, after seventeen years, the cicadas are probably stirring. Eek.

My beat-up copy of the *American Heritage Dictionary* serves as an ersatz Bible, and it's on my lap. If I look up a word that sends me to the appendix, I find a bit of human history. "Happy," for instance, once meant "luck." Not good luck or bad, just luck. Look what we have done to ourselves. We think we can actually *pursue* happiness.

I look up "certainty" because I live with uncertainty. Where did it come from? Earliest meanings: to sift, separate, decide. Not much help. I look up "mortal," a word I have always loved because it sounds so gentle, and find to my horror that one of its earliest roots is "goblin." Scratch that.

I give up and think perhaps now is the time to finally organize the jumble in my cupboards. (Sift, separate, decide.) Ten minutes later my counters are covered with stacks of saucers and bowls and mugs and glasses and a wooden berry picker and old vitamins I never opened and two different espresso makers and one French press and a few Lego creations plus a pinecone, two hair bands, and a very old chocolate bar. I don't know what to do next, so I leave it all on the counter and go back to the couch next to Carolina, who is still snoring. I consider taking a nap myself, but instead I rally and decide to vacuum the living room, puzzled and slightly alarmed by the loud clicking sounds, wondering what the hell is getting sucked up (Legos coins ciggybutts), but I keep vacuuming and what runs through my mind instead of wisdom is *Smoke 'em if you got 'em*, which is no way to live even if it is a metaphor. That's what I get for trying to think deeply.

So I drive to Chuck's house. His big dog, Pojd, is lying on the warm driveway, and she wakes right up because she loves me and thinks perhaps I am carrying something good to eat. Then there is Chuck in a clean white shirt. "I'd offer you tea but I don't have any," says Chuck.

"I've come for wisdom," I say, and he says, "Then you might as well leave right now," or words to that effect.

"I need to write about something big," I say. "I need to figure out how to live with uncertainty."

"You've been doing that your whole life," he says.

"I looked up 'certain,' and it only meant 'sift, separate, decide.'"

"Useless," says Chuck.

"I know, and then I looked up 'mortal.' Guess what it meant. 'Goblin.'"

"Also useless," he says, and we talk about how hideous that word is, capable of sending shivers up the spine. "It sounds so much like 'gobble,'" says Chuck.

Now we are sitting in his screened-in porch. An azalea has exploded into a froth of magenta right outside. Pojd puts her head on my lap and I stroke her silky ears.

"I'm afraid of people I love dying before I do. I need to find a way to live with that. I need to come to some conclusion. Words to live by or something. A mantra."

"Death is both a certainty and an unknown," Chuck says. "It's hard to get a grip on it."

"I love that," I say, writing down "certainty" and "unknown."

"And you can't deal with it when you're at a remove," he continues. "You need to clear a path. What you need is a new approach."

And with the word "approach," something falls into place.

Behind my studio, hidden by the forsythia and a field of stinging nettles, is a quarter acre of beautiful, almost spooky land. The silence there feels almost holy. The trees are tall and the light filtering through is green, the ground covered with myrtle and branches and nature's other debris. One enormous tree, felled by a recent hurricane, lies with its roots exposed, small creatures exploiting the decay. Once or twice I have picked my way through to this hidden place, but the nettles are waist-high and footing is uncertain. I should hire someone to come with backhoes to clear away the brush and snarl and tangle so I can look into the more mysterious place. I tell Chuck.

"It's a place to stand," I say. "And maybe that's the approach."

"And you don't want to sift and separate and decide," says Chuck. "You want a view of the whole wild mess."

So there is no conclusion, but it feels like one anyway.

"Because it's worth looking at," says Chuck.

Vacation

M om," says Catherine, when I tell her of my plans for plowing up the forsythias. "Mom, maybe you should save that money for a vacation." Catherine wants all of us to go away together somewhere hot with blue water and child care. All-of-us makes a big package, but Catherine has dreamed of this since her treatment began. We never get around to it. It's not that we lack the will. We have the will. We lack the money and the follow-through. Real life is always in the way. But somewhere an island is dancing in the sun, waiting for us to get our act together. There are palm trees and turquoise water and blue sky and white sand, and everyone is safe.

The End

I wish that when the time comes we could all join hands and rush into the surf together.

Back Window

My friend Maya gave me the back window of her old Land Rover, complete with windshield wipers. "24447CS" is scrawled in yellow highlighter on the glass. The window has been in my studio for more than a year as I try to decide what to paint on it. What is behind us?

I decide to paint nothing. Grabbing a rag and some soapy water, I plan to keep it clean.

Love

Love can accommodate all sorts of misshapen objects: a door held open for a city dog who runs into the woods; fences down; some role you didn't ask for, didn't want. Love allows for betrayal and loss and dread. Love is roomy. Love can change its shape, be known by different names. Love is elastic.

And the dog comes back.

Acknowledgments

Thank you first, and always, to my family. You know who you are. You are my life. Special thanks to Catherine and Tim for placing their trust in me.

Ann Patty, you made me do it. Your help and encouragement kept me at it. Thank you.

Luis Jaramillo, Heather Abel, Alison Hart, and Matthew Brookshire, thank you for our many writing weekends and glorious feasts. (Where's that cookbook?)

Thank you also, Michele Mortimer, for your early support and reassurance.

Thank you, Hannah Verrill, for your open heart, and Bar Scott, for your friendship.

Robin Desser, Pam Dorman, Elisabeth Scharlatt, and Dan Frank, your kind words meant the world to me. Still do.

A thousand thanks to Nan Graham, for your thoughtful input and enthusiasm and support. I am beyond grateful. Thank you, Kara Watson, and all those at Scribner who helped in so many ways to make this a book. I appreciate everything you've done.

To the Oncology Support Memoir Workshop: Carol Dwyer, Blaze Ardman, Nancy Henry, Dean Lavin, Roberta Jehu, Kathy Burgher, Suzanne Dean, Juliet Harrison, Annie La Barge, Marjorie Leopold, Craig Mahwirt, Marge Roberts, Sharon Stonekey, Barbara Sarah, Phyllis Silvers, Micky Shorr,

Robert Smith, and Ruth Wahtera. What can I say? You let me into your lives. You gave me the grit to finish this book. You show me how to live.

Finally, a special thanks to Stephen Dobyns, for a reason apparent to anyone familiar with his striking work.